AF429035

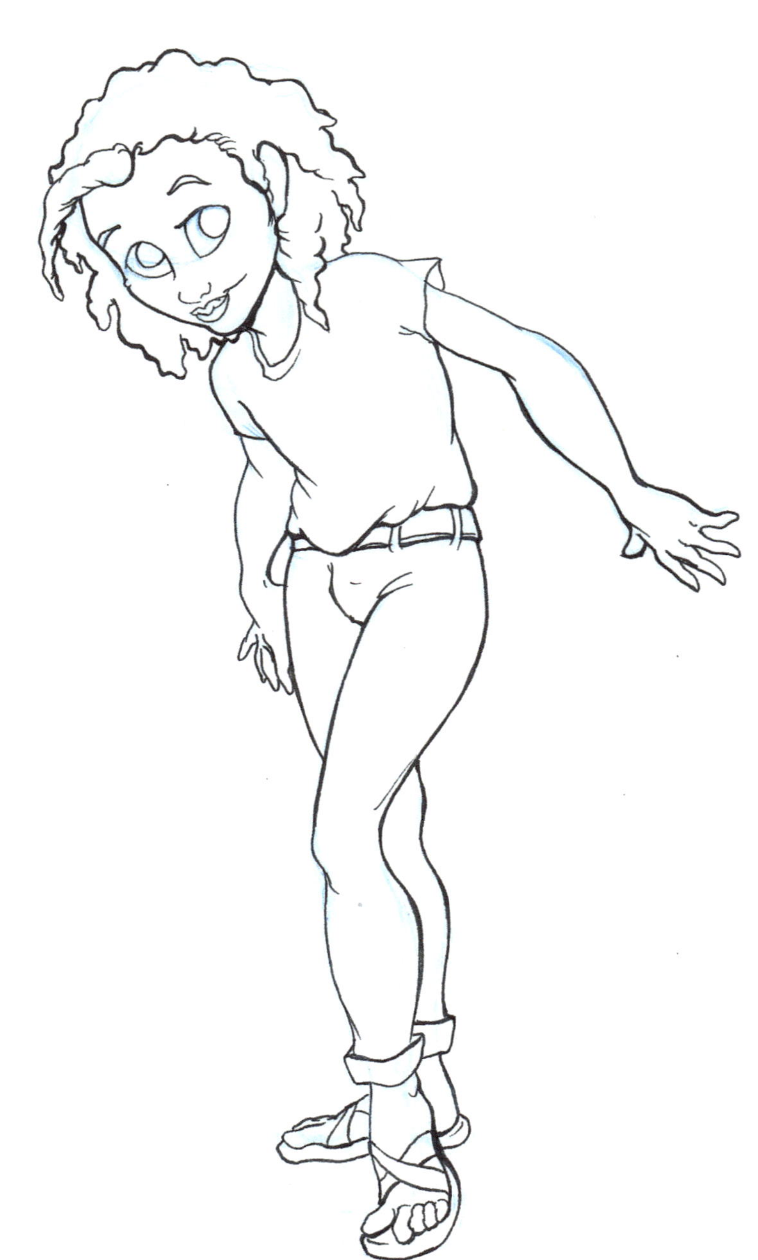

Making a Graphic Novel

10 (easy-to-follow)
Steps That Made the
Dream of Jaydi's Story
a Reality

by Alicia Dianne

Contents

Introduction: Start Here!

In this book, I relay my personal experience through the process of making my first graphic novel, *Jaydi's Story: In the Beginning*. Much of my experience involves my own faith and subjects on religion. I'd like to say that I respect and understand that your beliefs and personal journey may look different from mine. My hope is that you see the process and notice the overall themes within each step and are able to apply them to your own life and creative process in a way that makes sense to you. Now, let's get started!

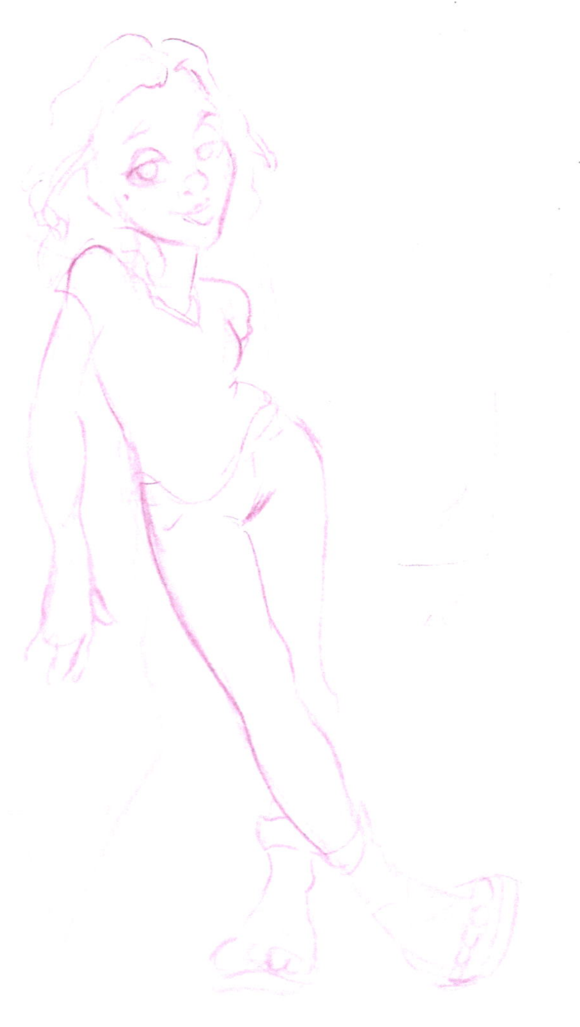

Early sketch of *Jaydi Asha*

Step 1: Get Inspired

I began *Jaydi's Story* in 2015. It was a time when I was going through a lot of life transition. I was still living in Albuquerque, NM and feeling very disconnected. I was, quite frankly, unhappy. Despite the struggles I was facing in my personal life, I was for the first time, really starting to grow my faith in a new way. I was listening to a lot of spiritual lessons and programming and came across an interview with Roma Downey, a talented actor and director, star of *Touched by an Angel,* as well as the producer behind such hits as *The Bible* miniseries, and *A.D.: The Bible Continues.* In the interview, Roma explains the incredible things that can happen when you pray the simple prayer, *"Use Me."* I found what she said compelling, so I decided I would give this prayer a try! I'd see what would happen and if God would actually answer. Well, He did! That night I spoke to God, I asked Him *sincerely,* truly with my heart opened, to *"use me."* What happened next for me may be hard for you to believe...

That very night I said that prayer, I had a dream. Which actually seemed more like a vision, because it was so incredibly *real*. I saw a girl. I didn't know the girl but I knew, somehow, that she was an *African* girl and that she was in terrible pain. Not physical pain, but deep emotional pain. Strangely enough, I could *feel* her pain. It was a heavy, intense weight in my chest, that of a deep spiritual mourning. I woke up before the first light, with my face completely covered in tears from crying in my sleep - an experience I had never experienced before or since. You couldn't believe my shock. Neither could I, because the first thing that came to my mind right there in my dimly lit bedroom... was to grab my sketchbook and I draw this girl. Somehow, I knew, right there in that moment, that I needed to record this girl from my dream.

Here is what I drew:

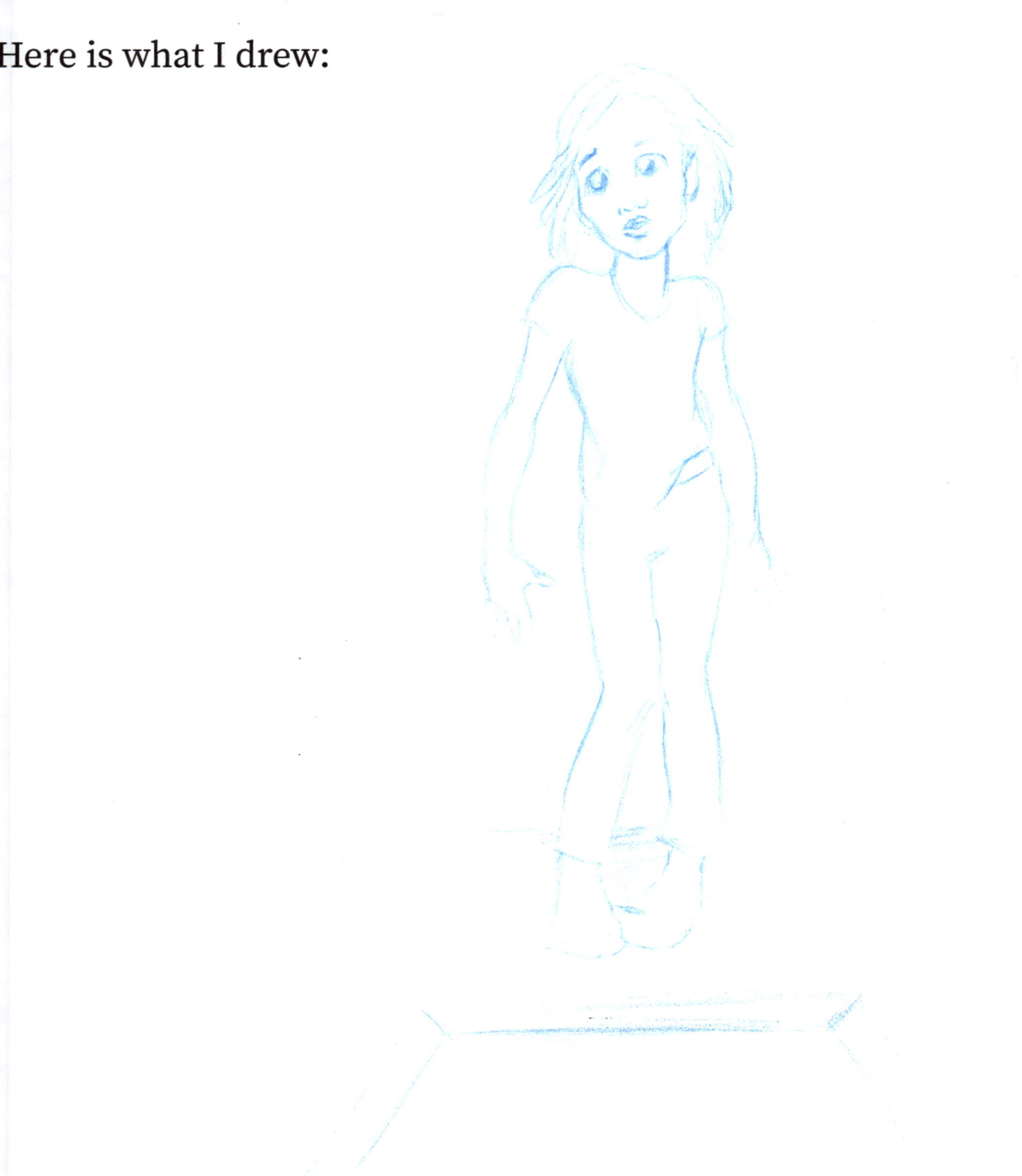

I also immediately got up out of bed and took a photo
of myself with my face still covered in tears. I still didn't
know what the dream meant, but I was about to find out.
That very Sunday when I attended church, the entire
service was dedicated to missionary...

I had never given much thought to missions up to that
point, but on this day, I was intrigued and I listened
intently. The pastors explained the all-new program
which involved international partnership. The partner
relationships would offer support in two locations
- which, honestly, could have been anywhere in the
world. Ironically, the first location mentioned was a small town in Kenya called Kwale.

This caught my attention immediately. And once they began going through the
photographs of the presentation, and I could see the people - I knew, without a shadow of
a doubt, that this was what the African girl in my dream was pointing me to.

I'd like to say it was easy after that. It wasn't. I still had no idea what I would be doing in
regards to Kenya. I certainly did not expect a graphic novel series to bloom out of this.
All I can say is, I was incredibly **_inspired!_** I was excited to learn more and to get involved
in any way that I could. From that moment on, I would seek out ways to learn about this
new subject matter through outreach, research, art making and character development

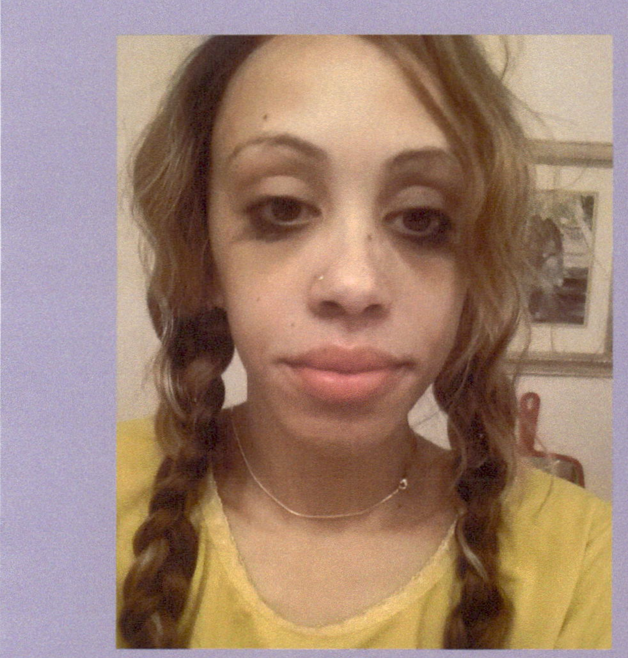

Myself after I woke up from the dream.
April 4, 2015

for something… But what? I didn't know,
yet I was inspired enough to follow the
breadcrumbs wherever they might lead!

*"Take the first step in faith. You don't have to see
the whole staircase, just take the first step."*
-Rev. Dr. Martin Luther King, Jr.

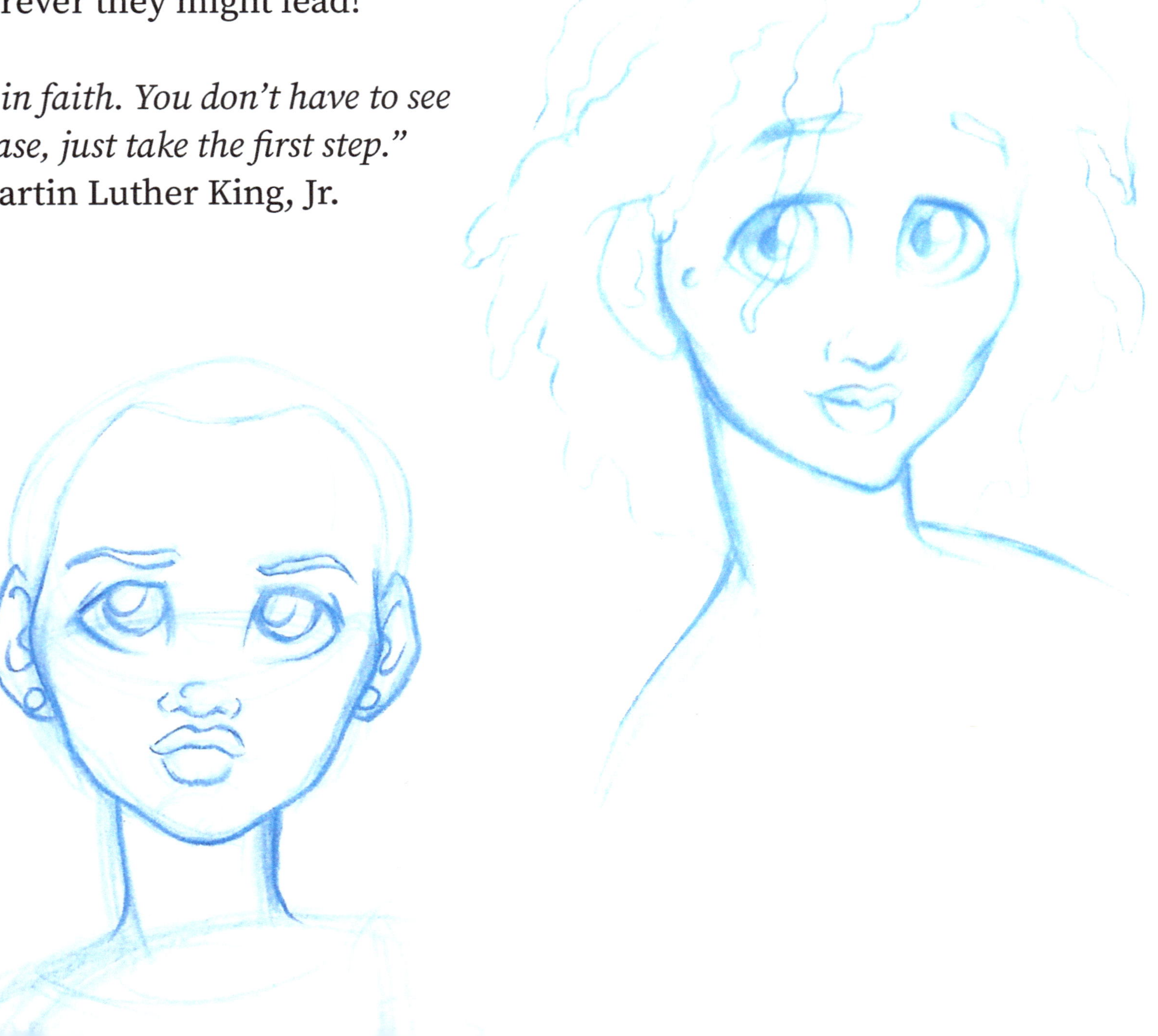

I didn't have much to start with on my own. All you really have to do is identify one step you can take now, in the present, that will lead you towards your inspiration. This is so important, so I will repeat it, **all you have to do is identify one step you can take now, in the present, that will lead you towards your inspiration.**

My first step? Reaching out to the missionary department and asking who I could speak with to learn more about their program. It was through this step that I was introduced

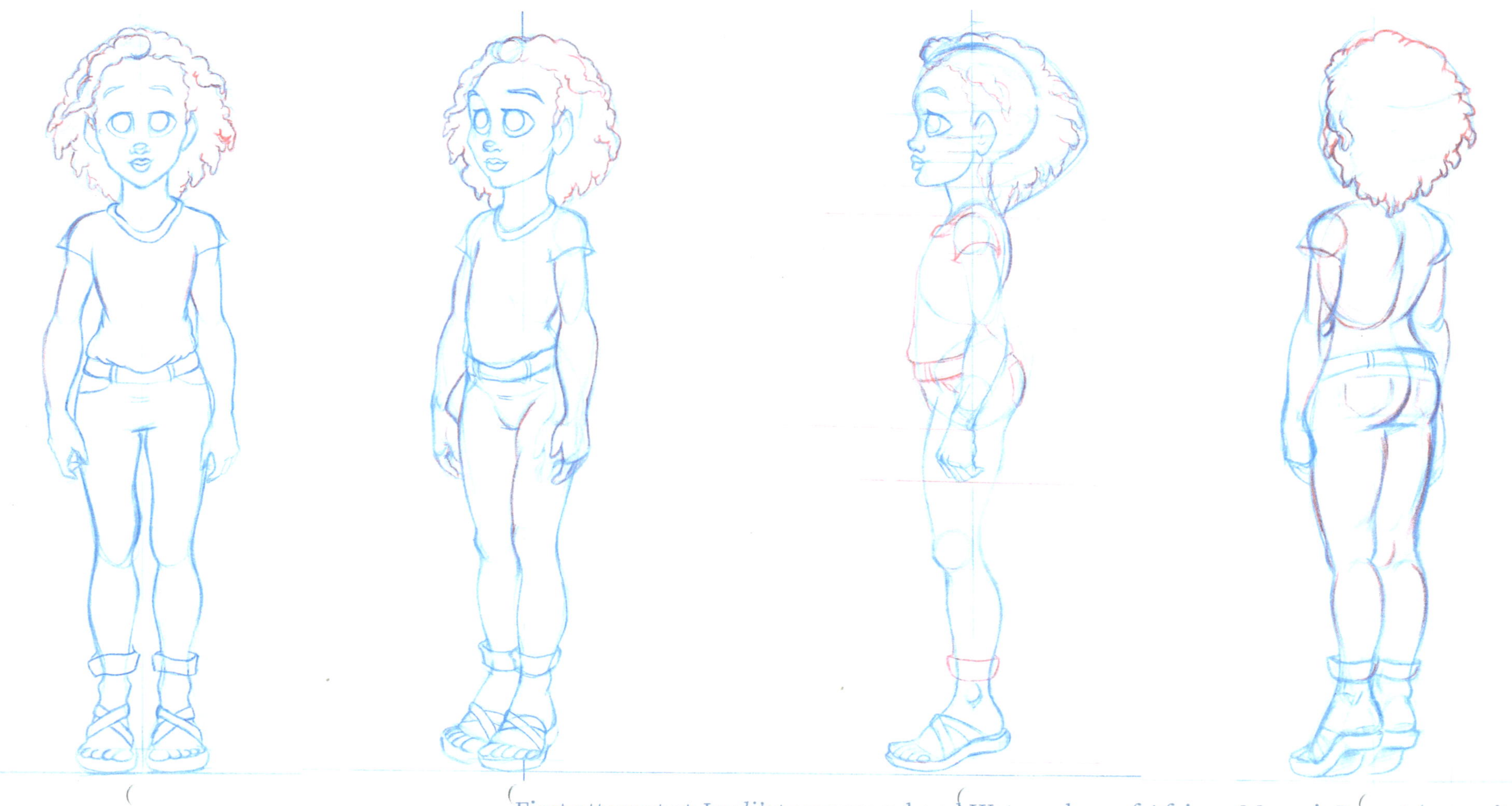

First attempt at *Jaydi's* turnaround and Watercolors of African Meyer's Parrot (opposite)

to a man named Bruce, the Missionary Director of my local church in Albuquerque. Through his kindness and openness, he was willing to sit down with me and tell me all about what their team was doing to fund medical clinics and provide educational supplies to the people of Kwale. He told me about the annual trips they'd begun taking to Kenya to work in partnership with a local organization in Kwale. Through our communication, he was able to offer me the more than 400 photos to view from their past year's Missionary trip. This allowed me see, meditate over and get inspired by the people, the location

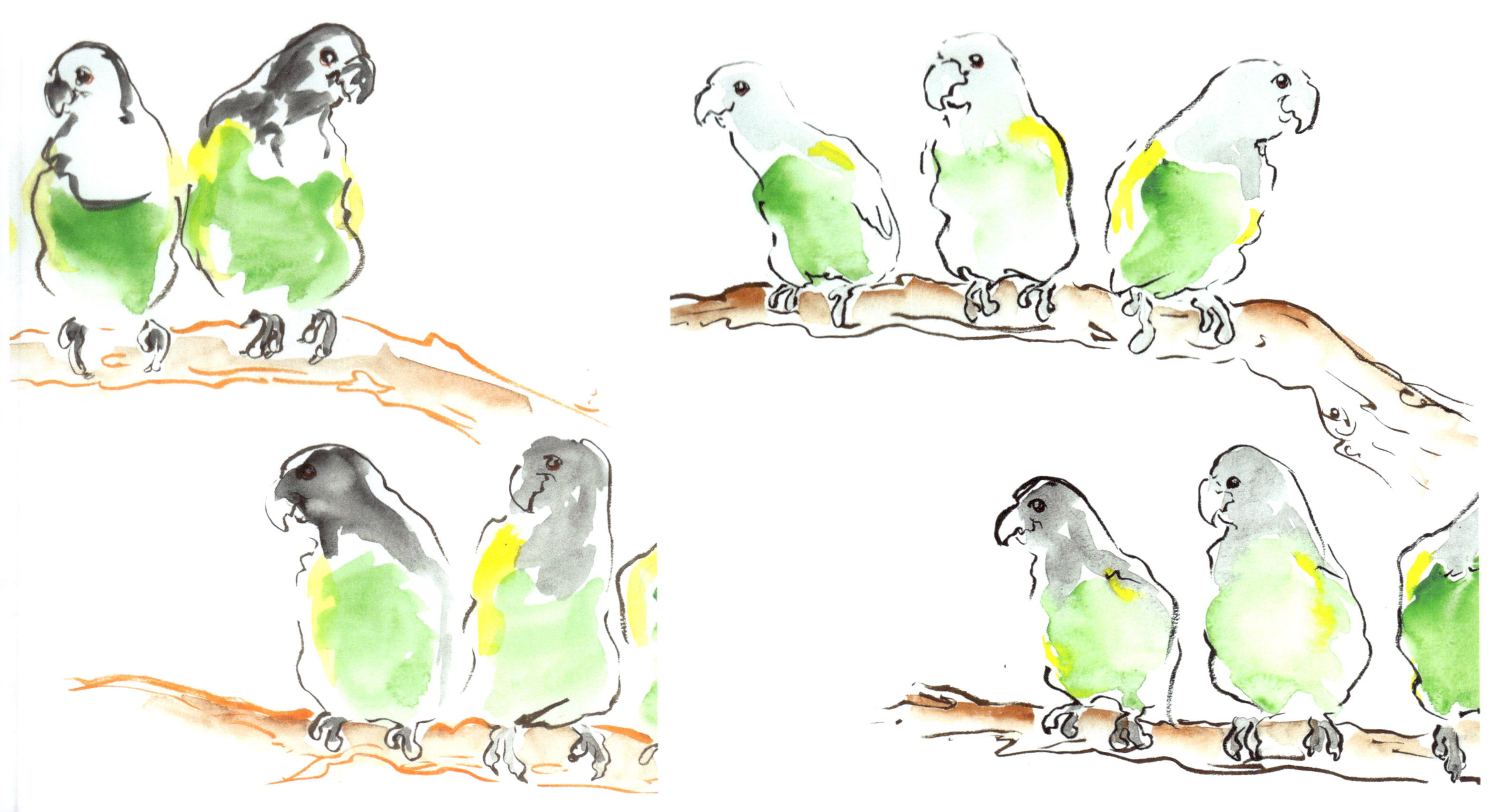

and the work being done. I did just that, the photos gave me lots of perspective - to see personalities, mannerisms, styles of dress and other intricacies that I might not have otherwise picked up on. Paying close attention to the structures, businesses, homes and imagery of everyday life, I was able to gain some sense of an actualization of a place I'd never been.

Get Inspired: Reflection Questions

1. What is a subject matter that peaks your interest that you've always wanted to explore in more detail?
2. What causes or social issues are you currently involved in?
3. What social or societal injustice do you feel emotionally invested in?
4. What is your ancestral country or continent of origin? How might you learn more about your own culture?
5. What are 3-5 steps you can take *now* to explore your newly discovered inspiration? Pick one and take action today!

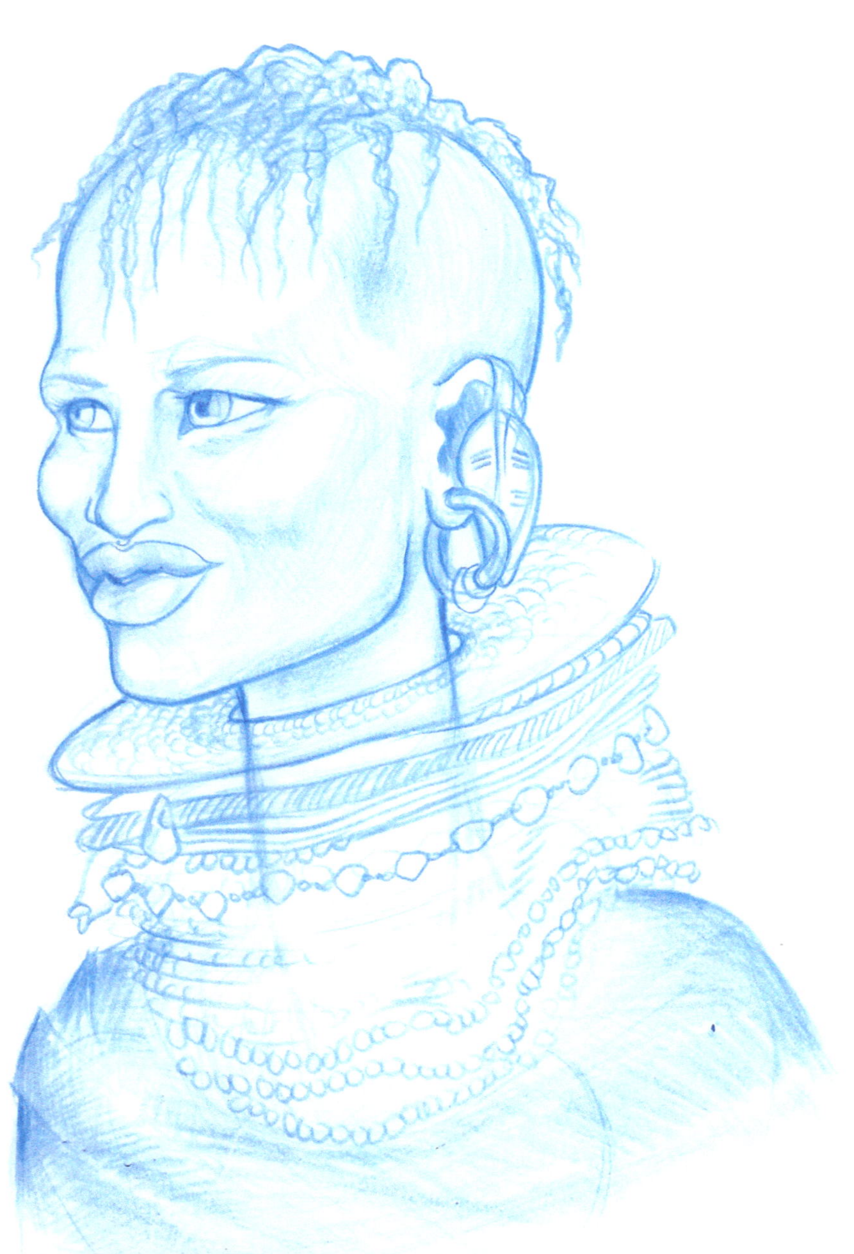

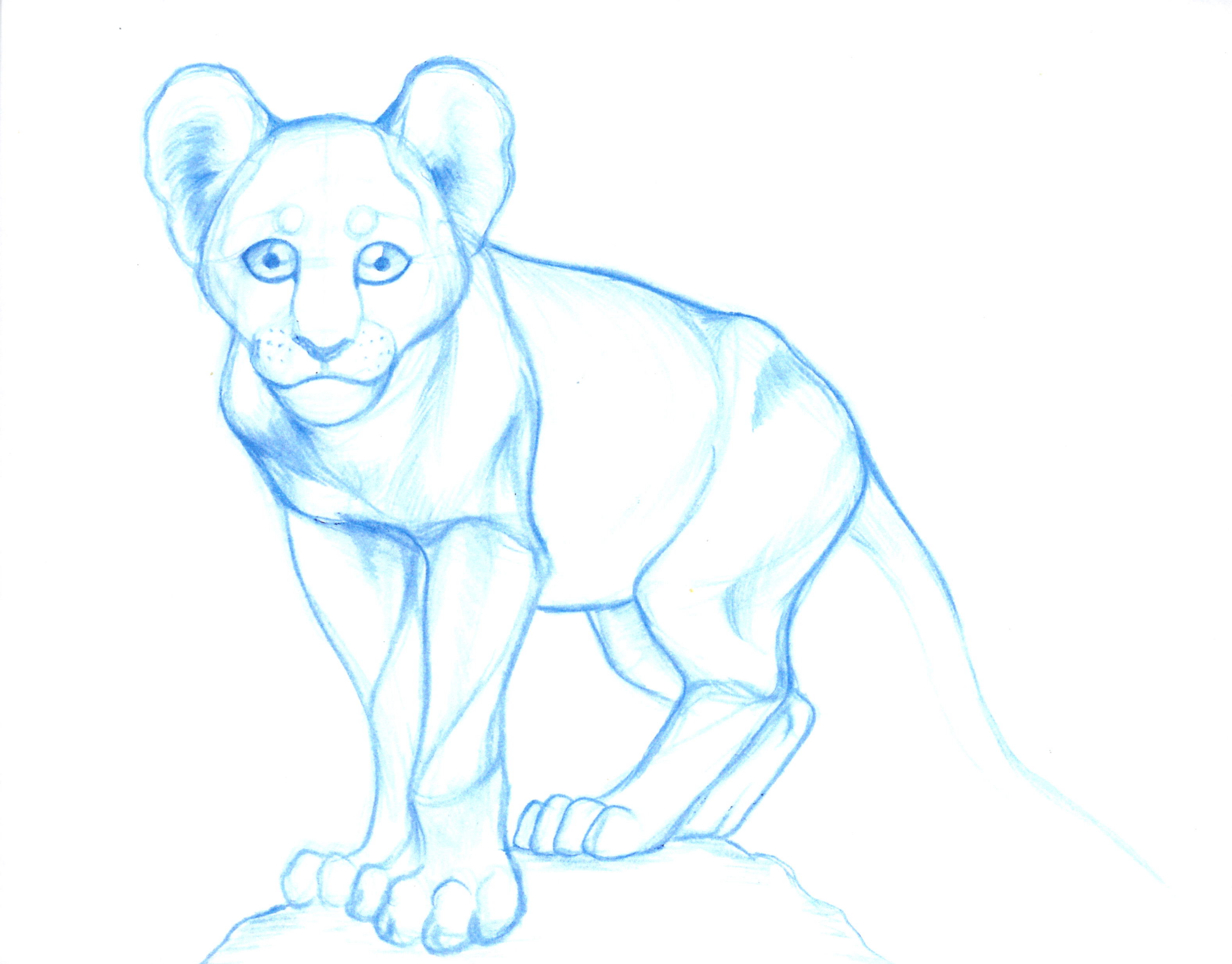

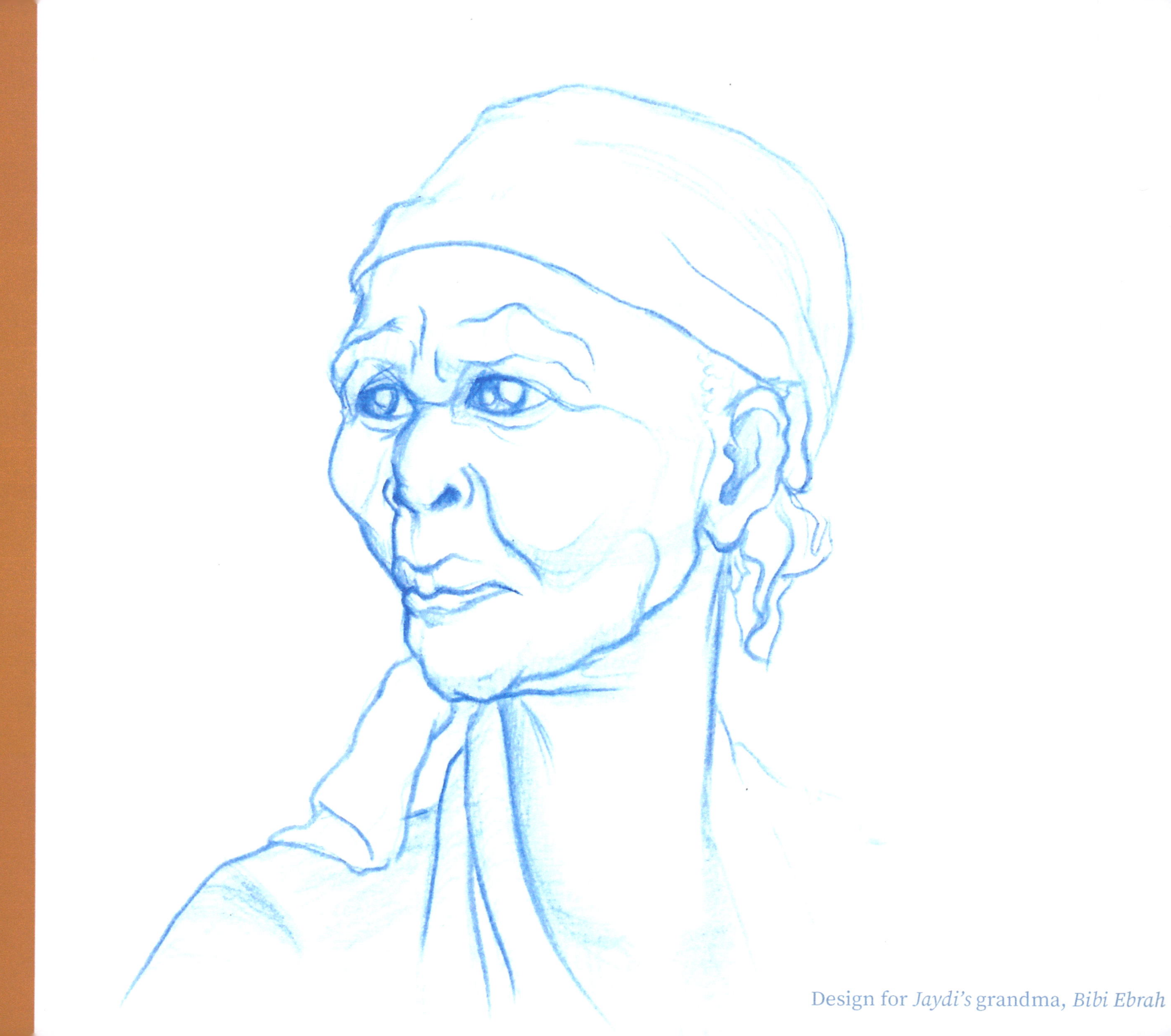

Design for *Jaydi's* grandma, *Bibi Ebrah*

Step 2: Discover Your Characters

The process of creating characters began with me, the reference photos and a little creative resource, known as a *character sheet*. A character sheet basically helps an artist or writer to create a character from the ground up by identifying in the blank spaces, aspects of the character's physical, relational and psychological attributes. Flaws and all, a character sheet allows one to explore and discover virtually all of a character's likes, dislikes, vices, internal struggles, greatest strengths and darkest secrets. Even if you may never write from those details directly, it can be incredibly powerful to be able to understand your character to the point that you can predict how they will react in any given situation, which allows you the freedom to write your character *as* your character! I've provided a character reference sheet for you to use in the **Resource List** in the back of this book.

Where can you draw inspiration for your characters? Just about anywhere! I've found that when creating my cast - many, if not all of my characters were inspired, if only in part, by the people I've known throughout my life. I drew back memories from my childhood. My friends, their parents, my teachers, mentors, and in one case even my mom's old boyfriend (in general, exes can be a great jumping off point for creating villains!) Seriously though, think first of your main character, your *Protagonist*, imagine that person up, give them a personality using a character sheet. Then from your main character, you should be able to imagine the type of people who might be around them. Who lives in their home? Who do they confide in? Who do they see everyday? Who gets on their nerves? All of these questions will allow you to **_discover your characters_**.

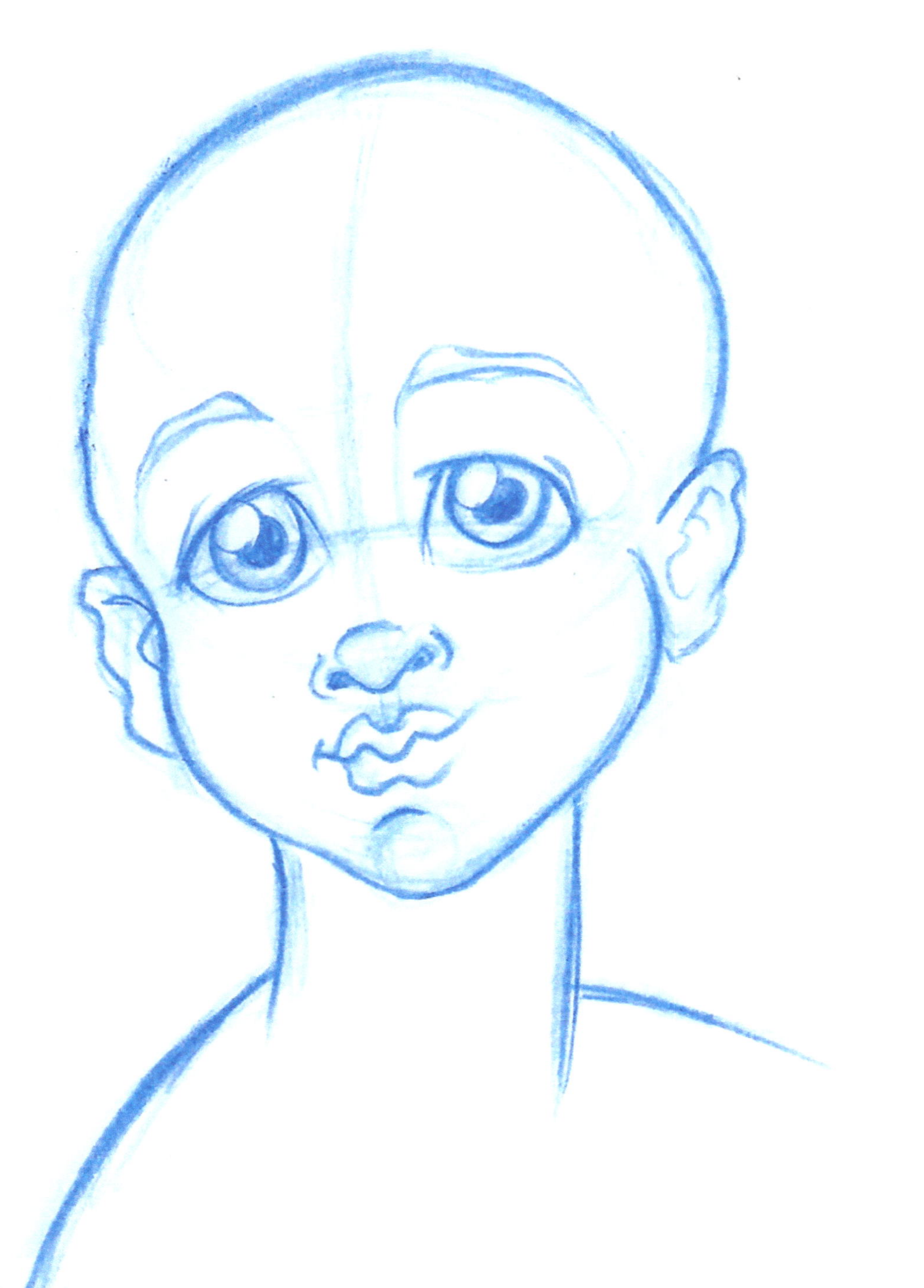

Design for *Jaydi's* brother, *Bandele*

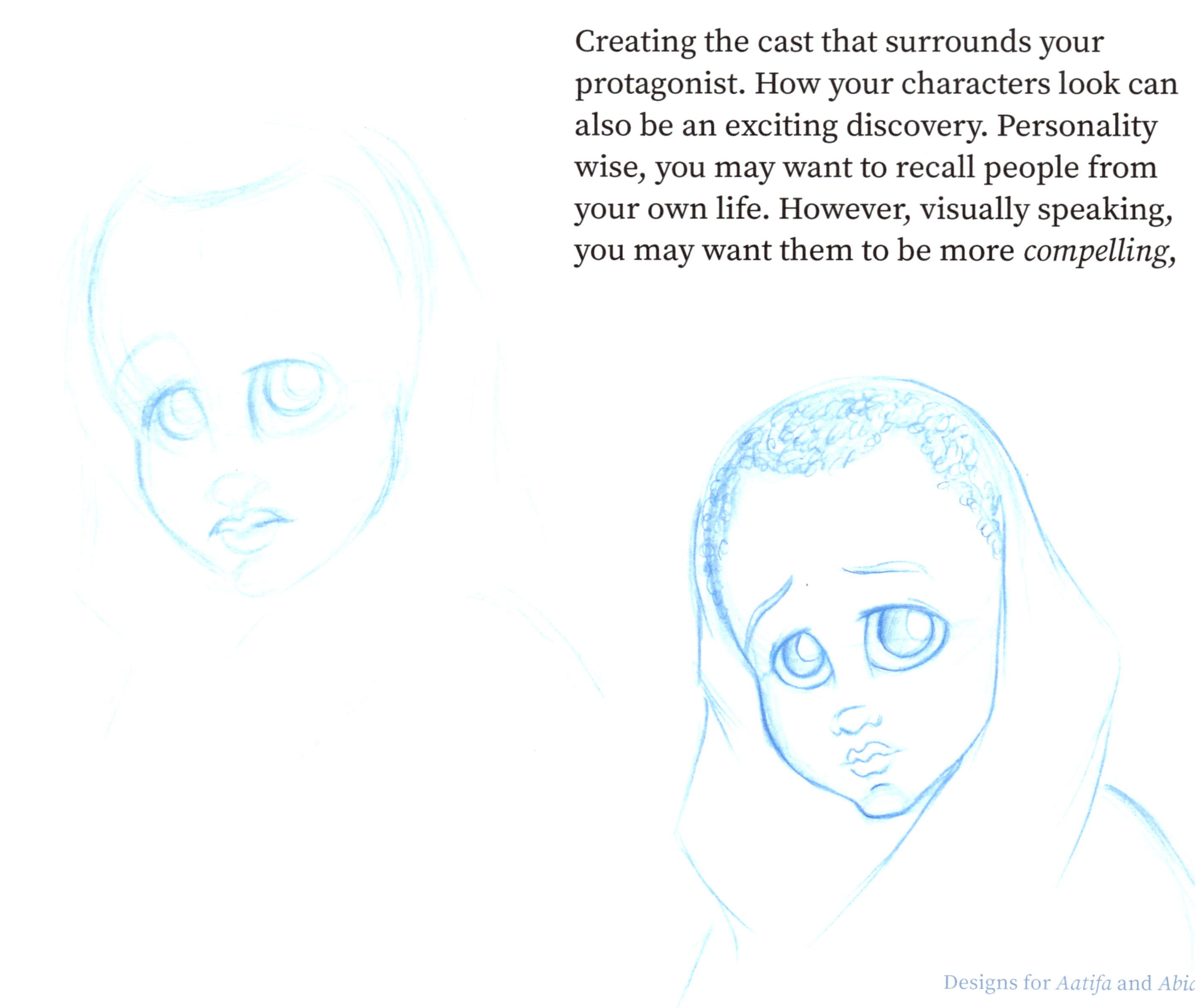

Creating the cast that surrounds your protagonist. How your characters look can also be an exciting discovery. Personality wise, you may want to recall people from your own life. However, visually speaking, you may want them to be more *compelling*,

you know, photogenic! My process for
this was a lot like casting for a movie.
I thought, if my graphic novel were a
live-action film, who would I want to
play the roles? I first used the photos
to scout interesting looking faces from
the region of my inspiration.

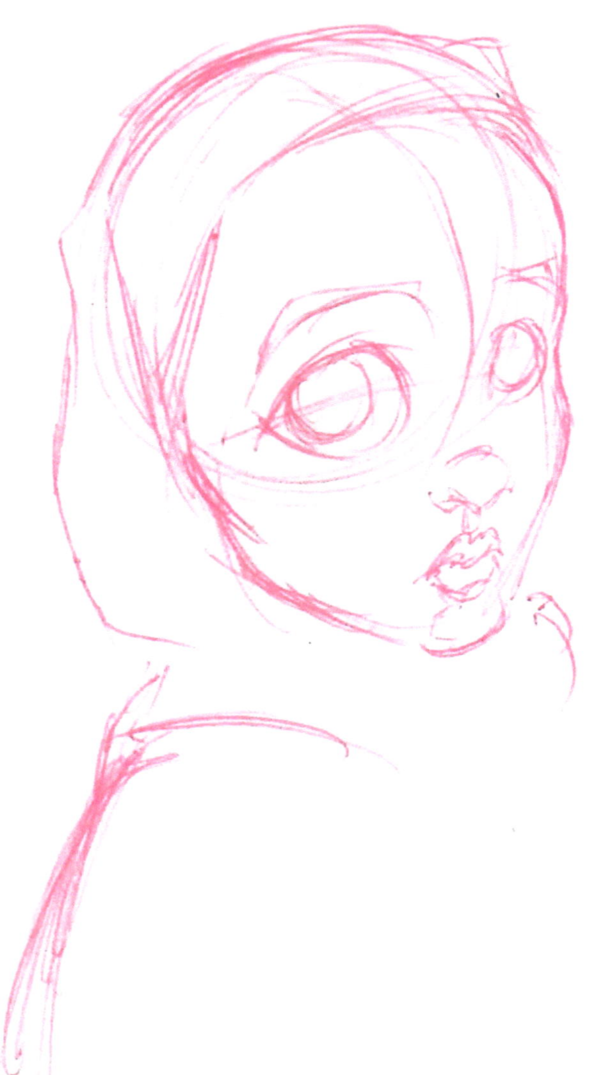

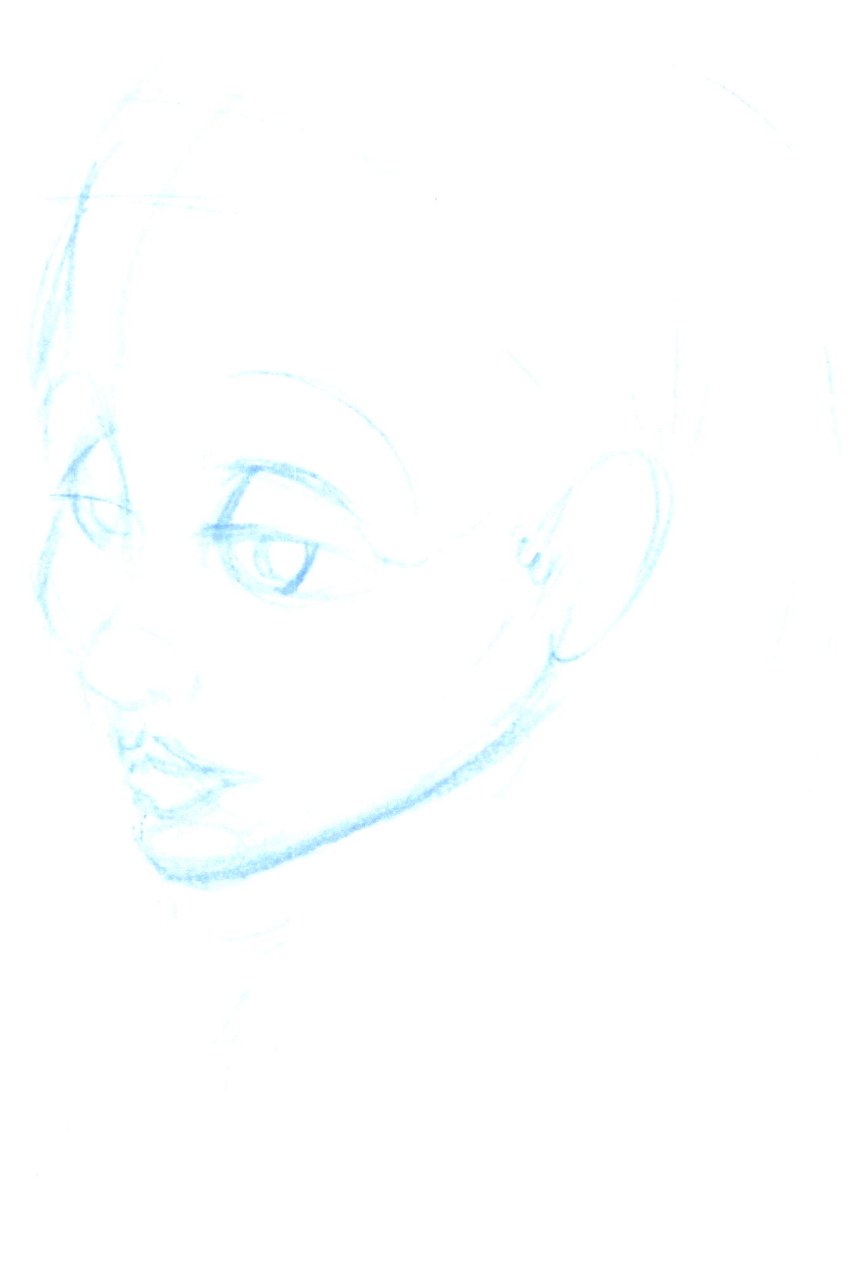

Then I selected real-life actors whom I felt would best play the parts. Next, I combined their looks and experimented to create the entirely new character variations who began to form my cast.

The process of naming can be a lot of fun too! Especially because I personally think all names should have a meaning, so I knew I wouldn't be picking them willy-nilly...

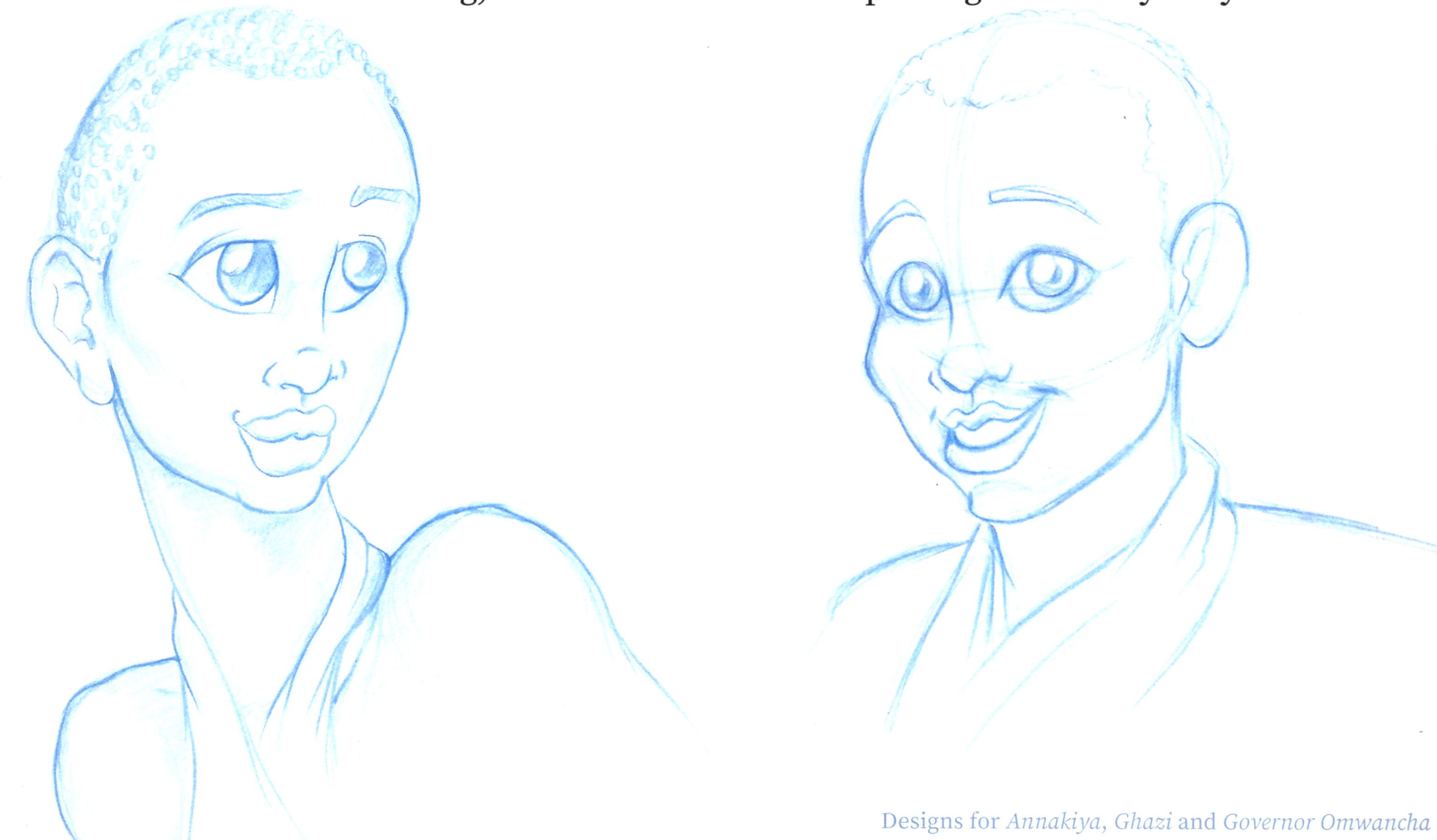

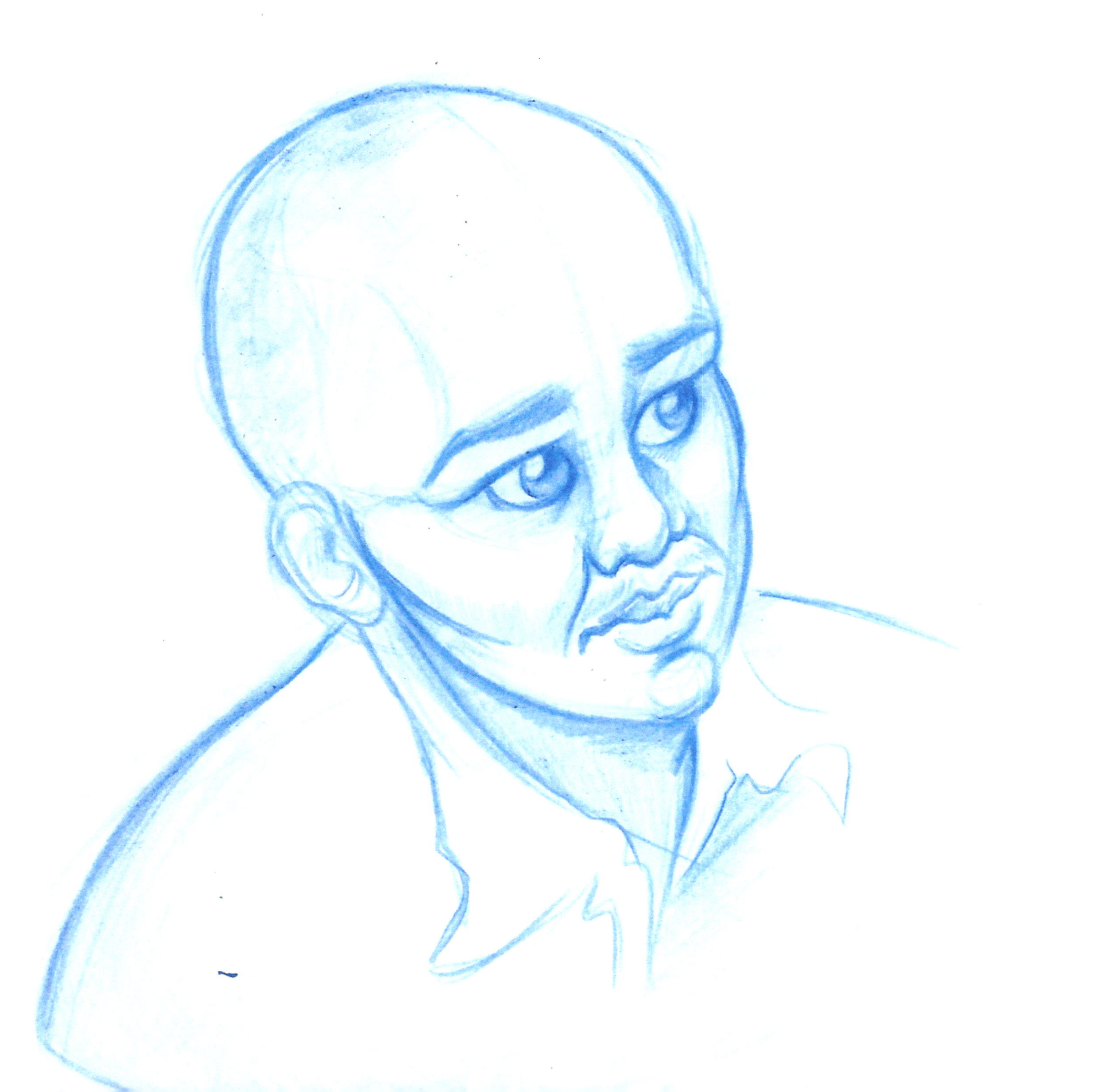

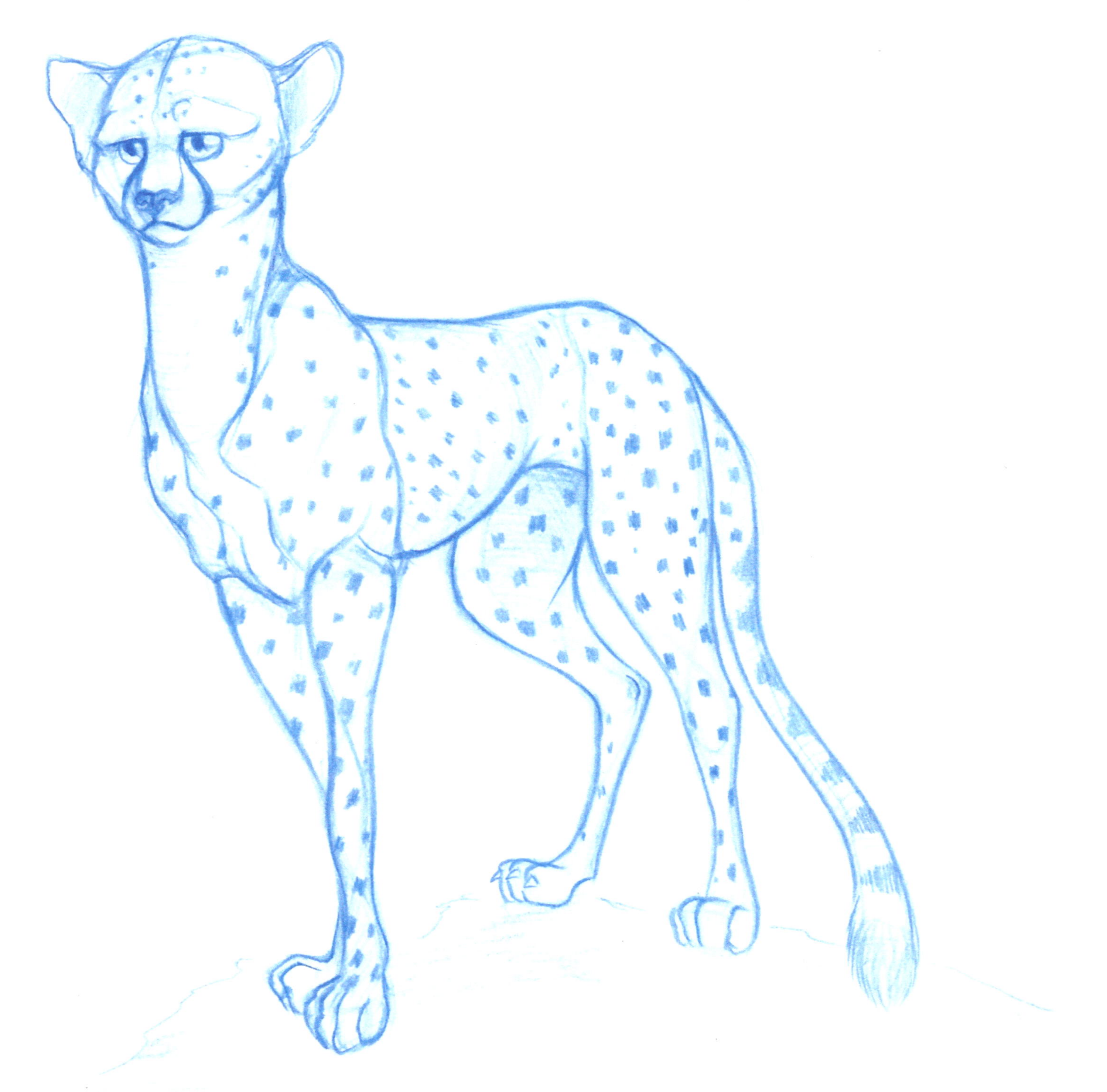

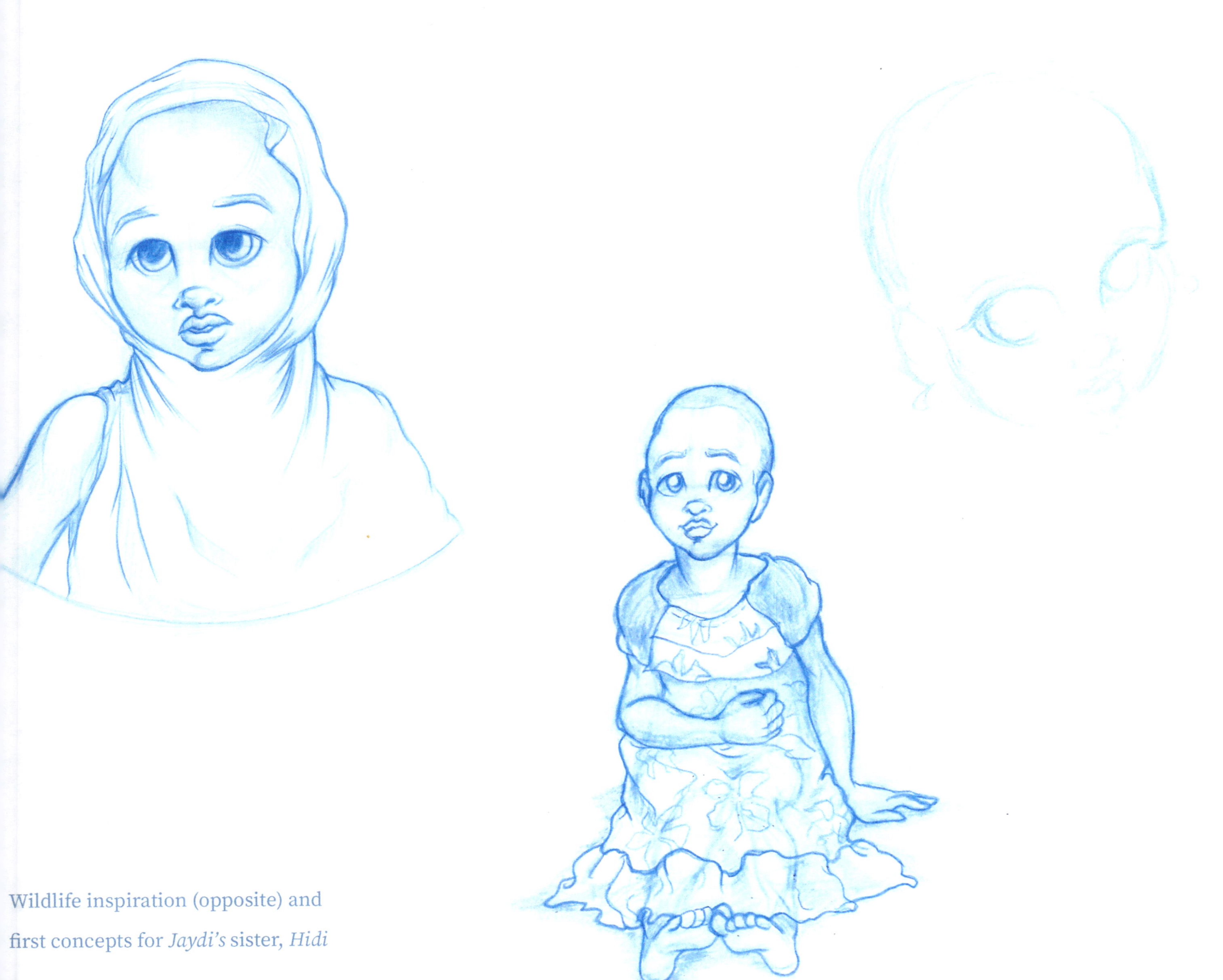

Wildlife inspiration (opposite) and

first concepts for *Jaydi's* sister, *Hidi*

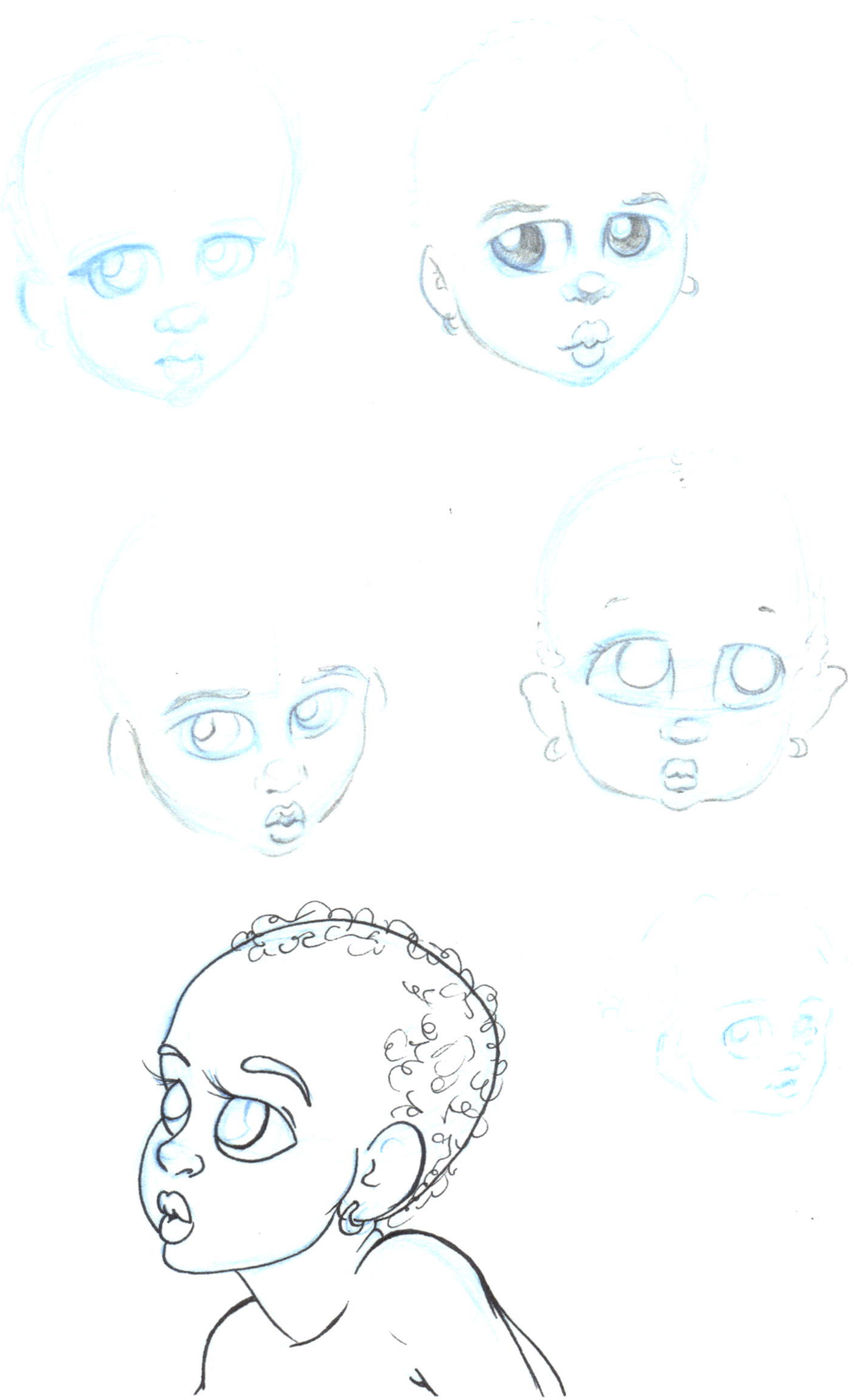

(although, *Willy Nilly* sounds like a great character name!) So where do you even begin to find meaningful names? One suggestion is to do what I did, which was a lot digging through Baby Name websites! This is a great resource that I've included in the **Resource List** because it allows you to search by masculine or feminine and in alphabetical order - say, if you can only think of the first letter you'd like for a character. It also will give you the origin of the name and most importantly, the meaning!

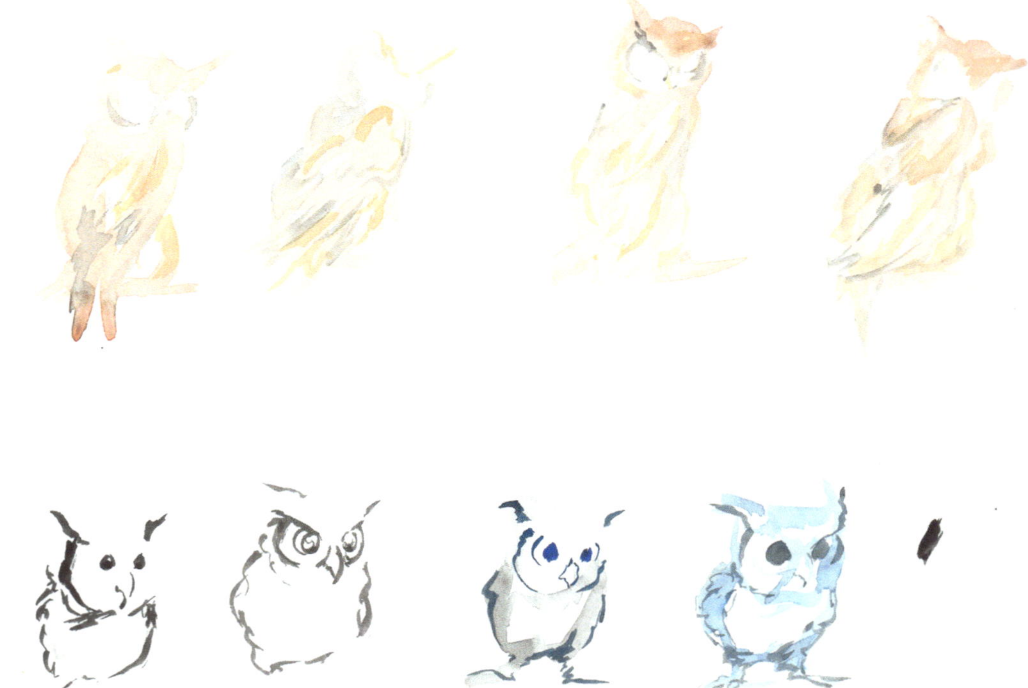

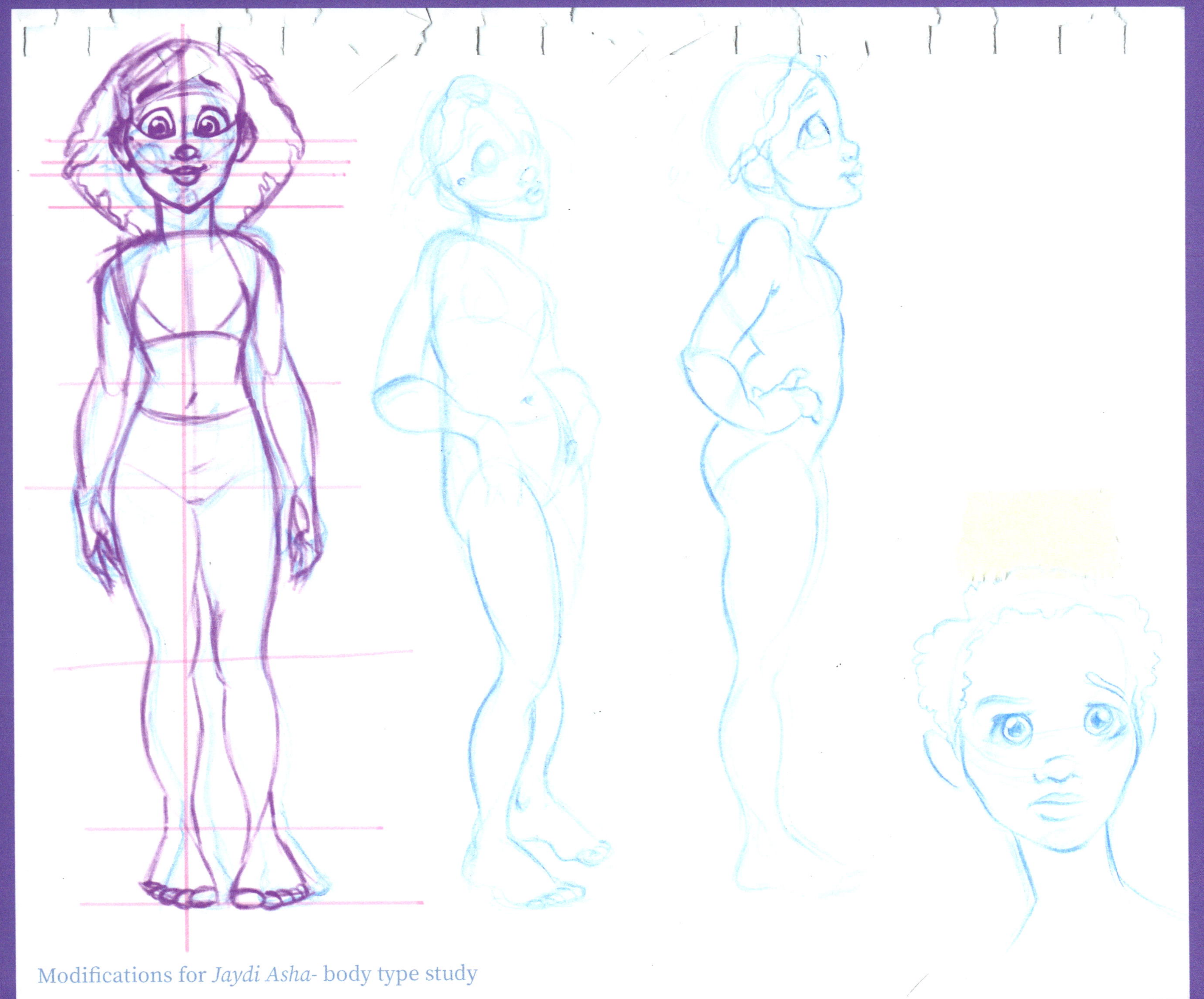

Modifications for *Jaydi Asha*- body type study

While naming the cast of *Jaydi's Story*, I looked through a ton of African baby names and their meanings. I also looked through surveys of popular names in East Africa, in an attempt to create a believable cast whose names also suited their personas. If you do take the baby name route, I'd recommend looking at more than one website, as the meanings and origins may vary depending on the source. When developing your cast, you can make your characters as wild and outlandish or as

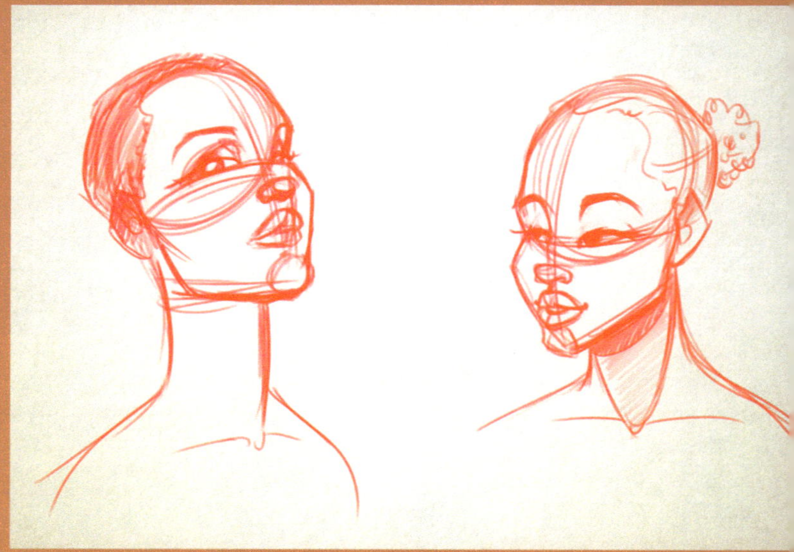

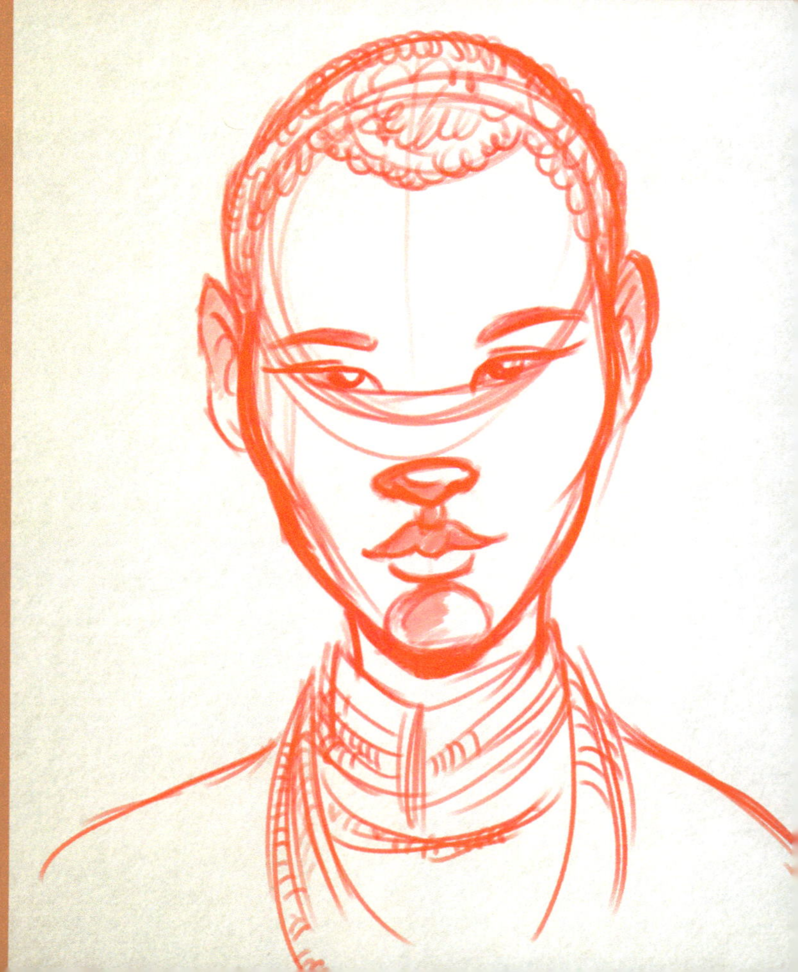

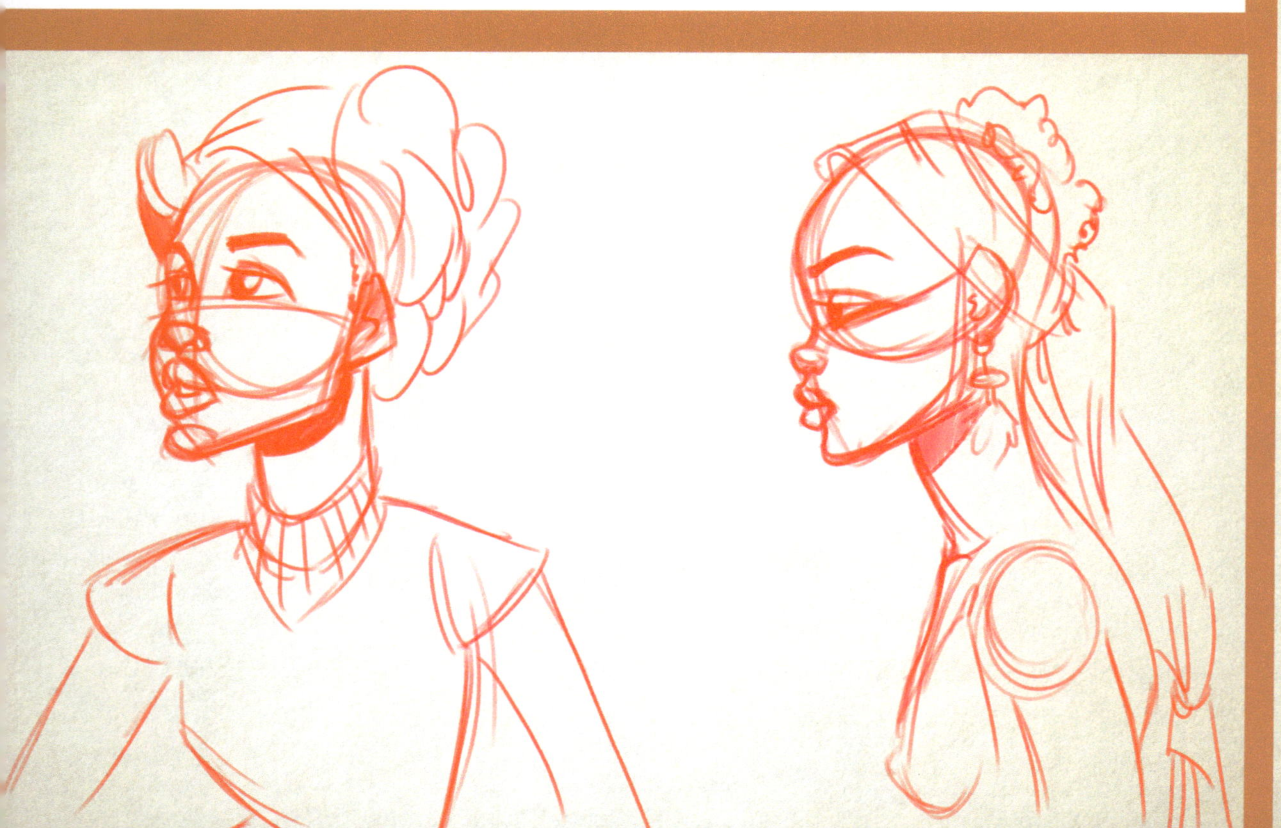

soft-spoken and shy as you like. My advice is just to make them *believable* to your story and create a wide variety of personas. Surprisingly enough, your main character is often very average! *Jaydi Asha Juma* is a simple girl dealing with a complex reality, but her best friend, *Sabrina Mwangi*, on the other hand, is very extroverted and can be unpredictable. This is a fun process, so let it be fun, and let your characters come to you!

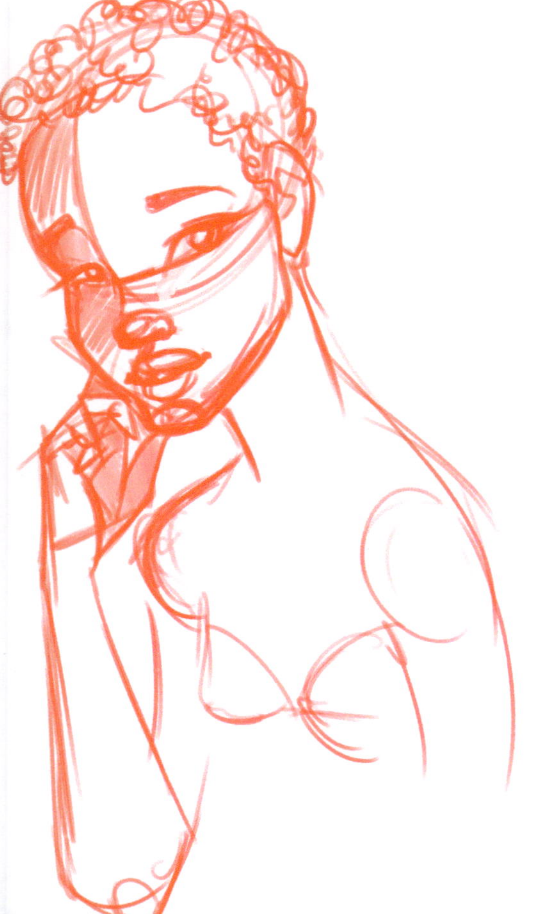

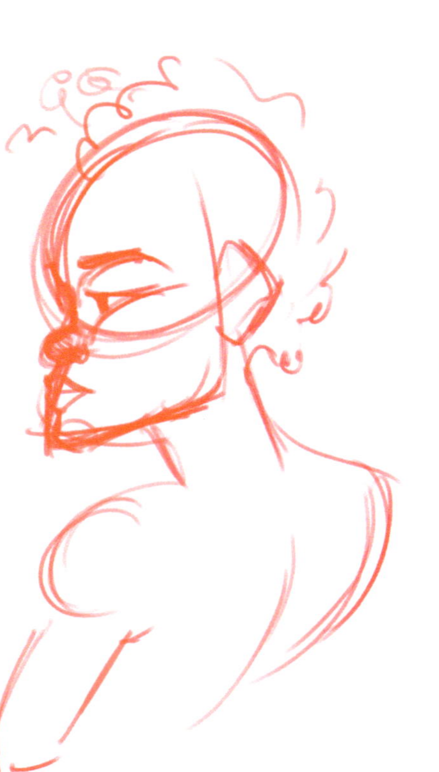

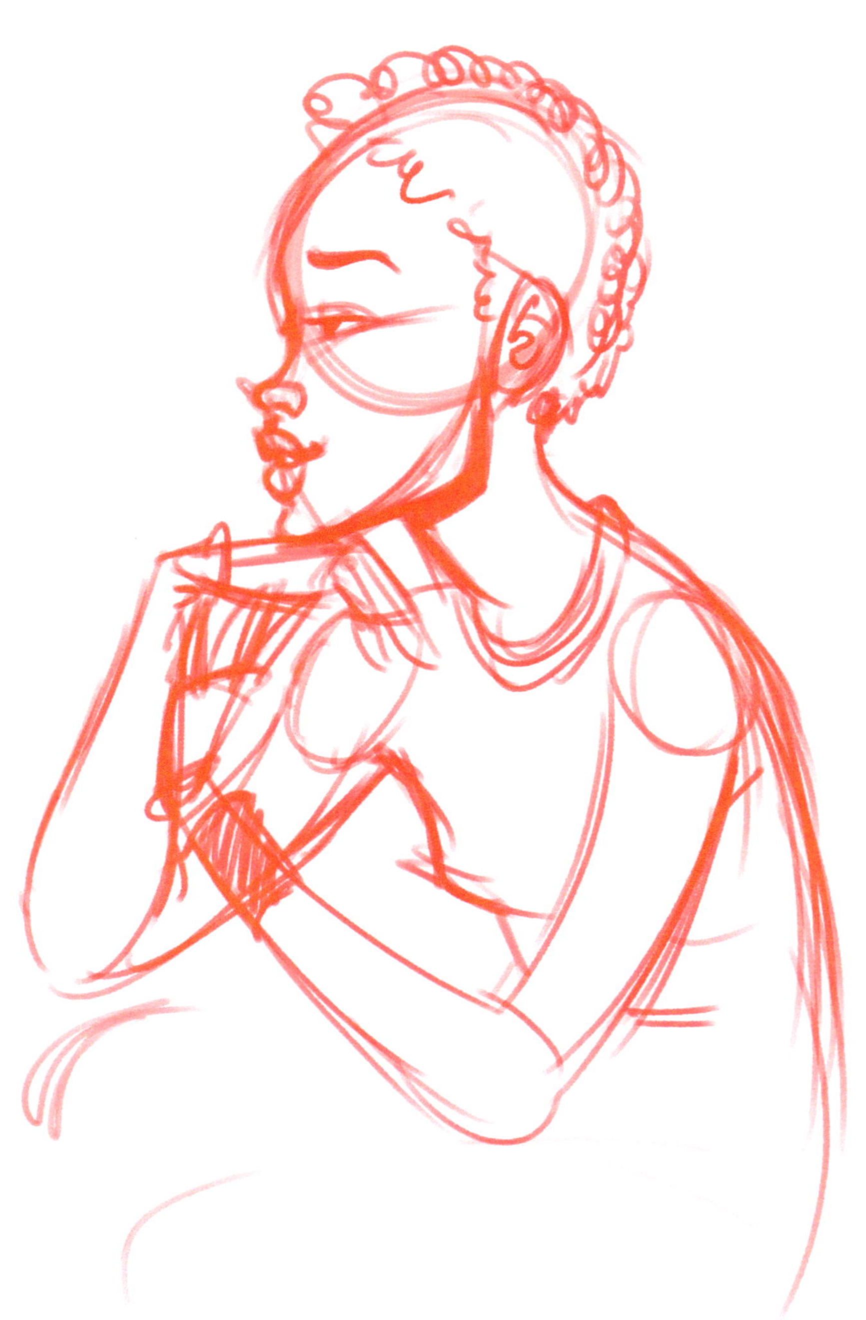

Discover Your Characters: Reflection Questions

1. Who is your main character? Fill out the *Character Reference Sheet* located in the **Resource List** in the back of this book to discover your protagonist, quirks and all!
2. Identify 3-5 people in your character's home or family life. Who do they live with? *Parents? Siblings? Aunts or Uncles? A partner? Children?*
3. Identify 3-5 people in your character's immediate circle. Who are their *friends? Neighbors? Peers? Co-workers?*
4. Is there an animal, pet or creature in your character's life? What animals are popular in your character's location? What lesser known animals exist in your character's environment? Could it be a fictional creature?
5. Who wants to make life *miserable* for your character? Create a character with a completely opposite world view as you protagonist. Meet your *Antagonist!*
6. Complete a *Character Sheet* for each character you decide will have a role in your story.

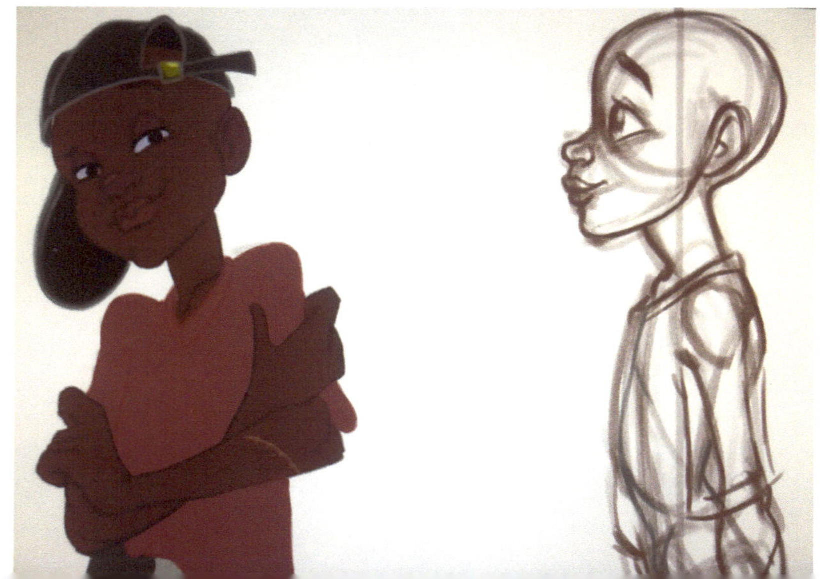

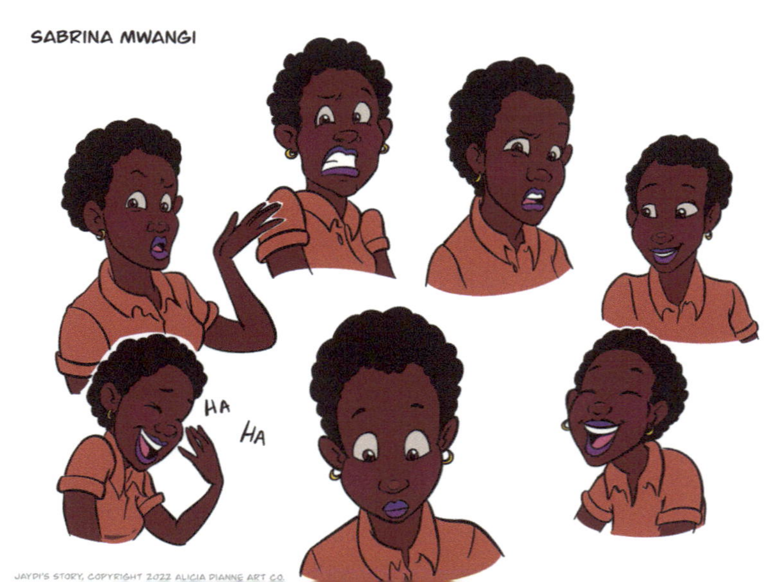

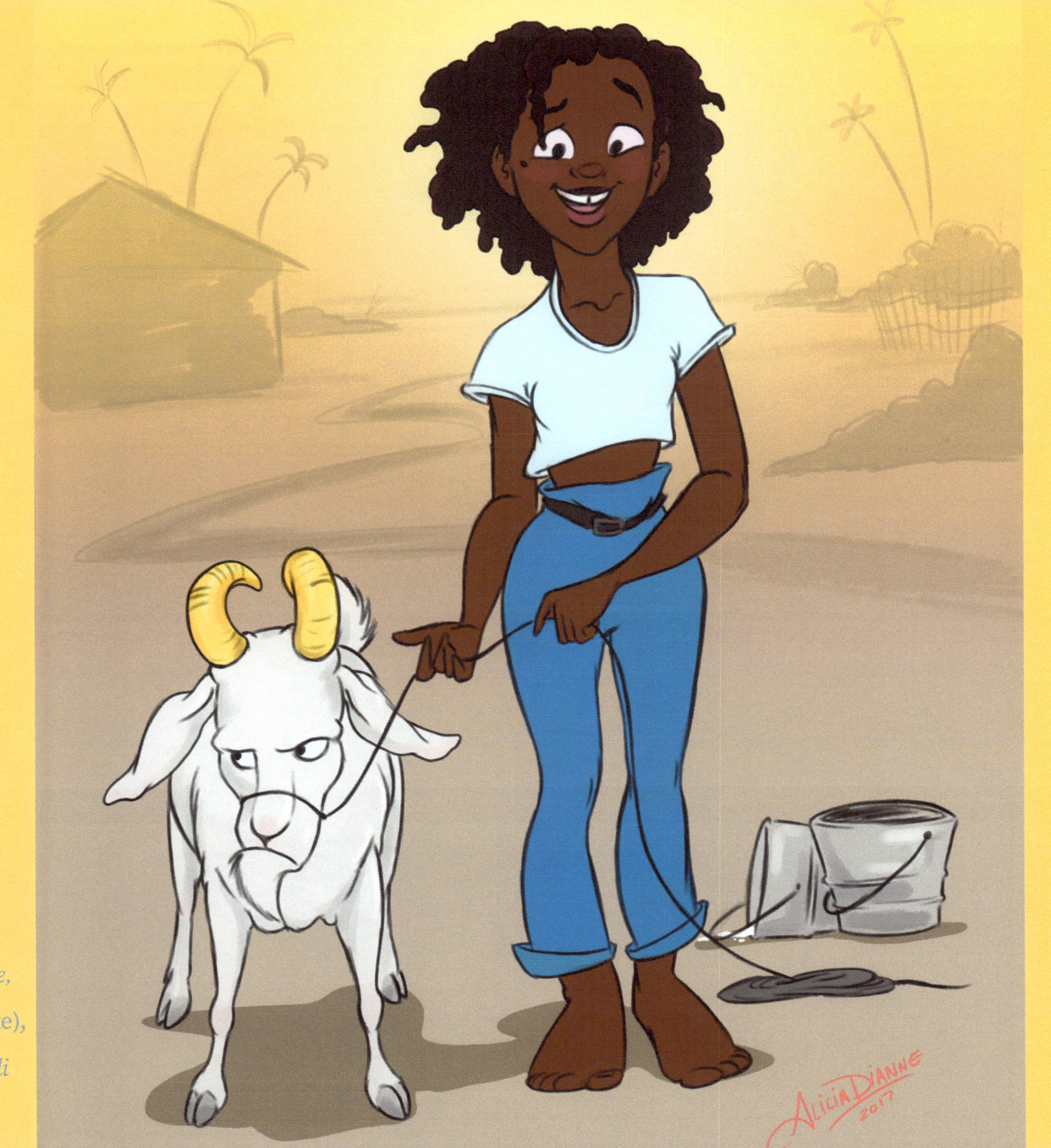

Refining Bandele, Sabrina (opposite), *Atsukpi* and *Jaydi* concept

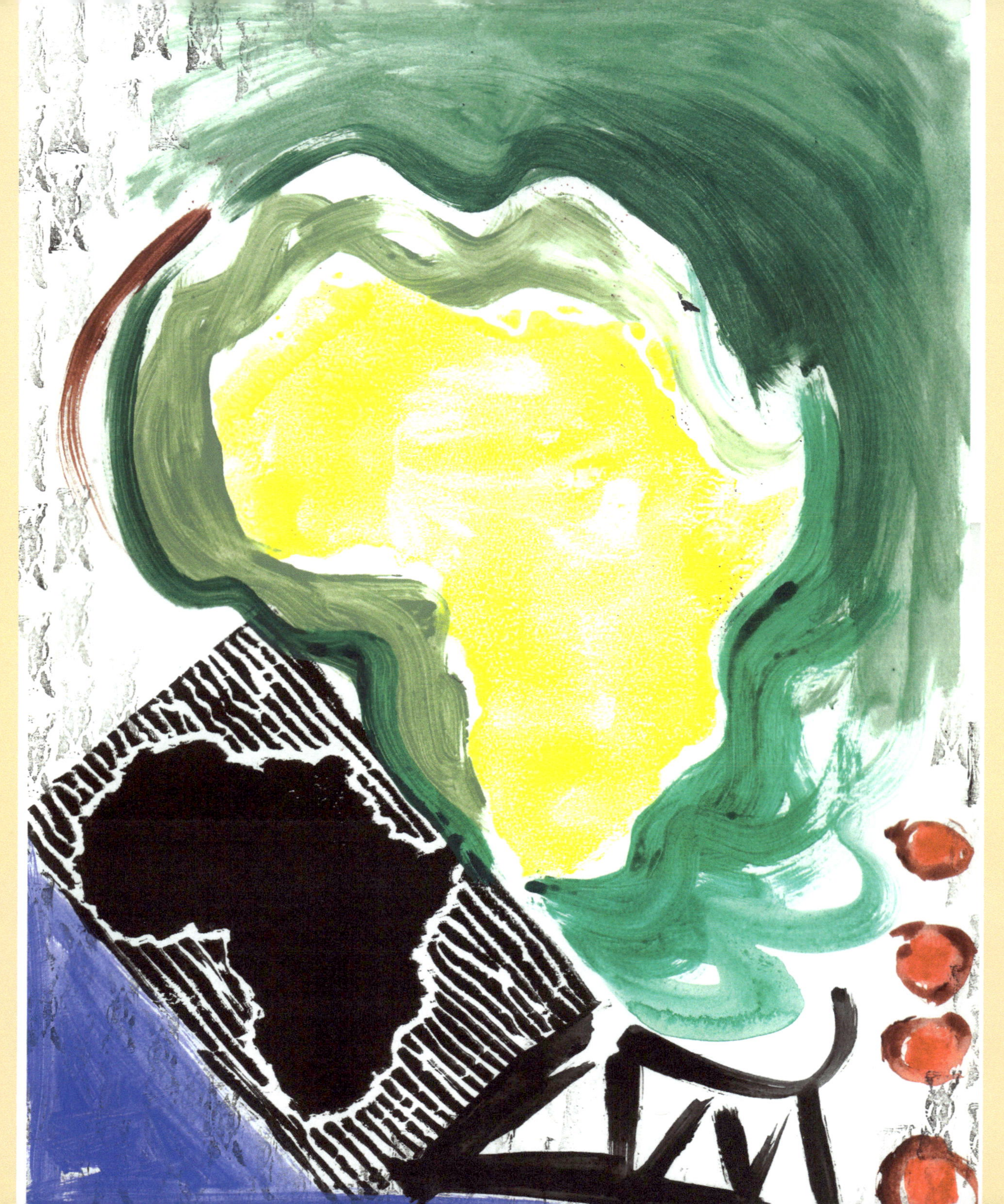

Step 3: Explore Art Styles & Uncover a Theme

Creating an art style involves lots of exploration. An ability that, for me, did not come naturally. In art school, I'd been trained to work and abide by many laws. Those being- the structure of a composition, the elements of design, the principles of animation, the rule of thirds and the undeniable physics of anatomy… I had never in my professional life, done much by the way of just *exploring*. This was until I met Diane.

Diane Rolnick is an *amazing* artist, and at the time that I met her in 2013, was a Continuing Education professor at the University of New Mexico (UNM). When I signed up for her *Experimental Drawing and Mixed Media* class, I had no idea what I was in for.

Experimental paintings based on African textiles

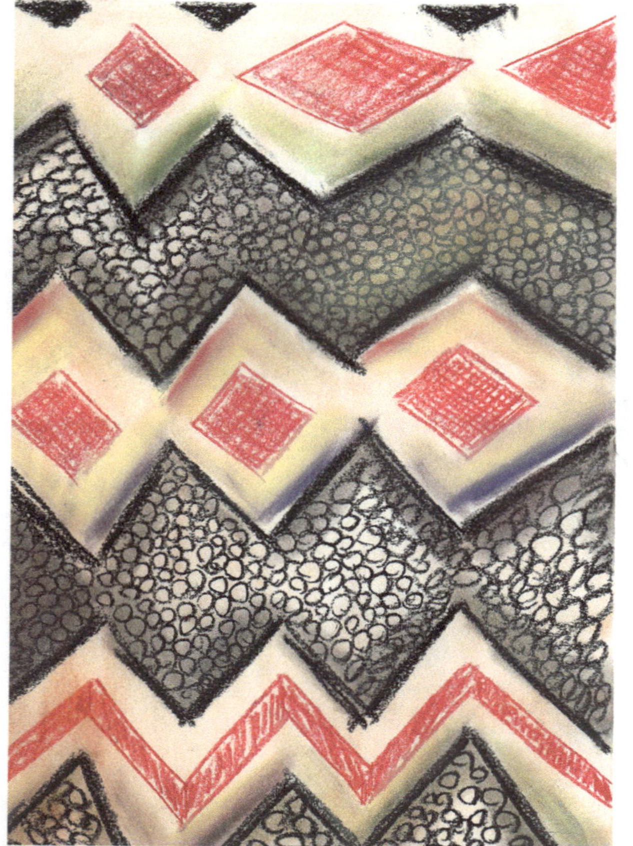
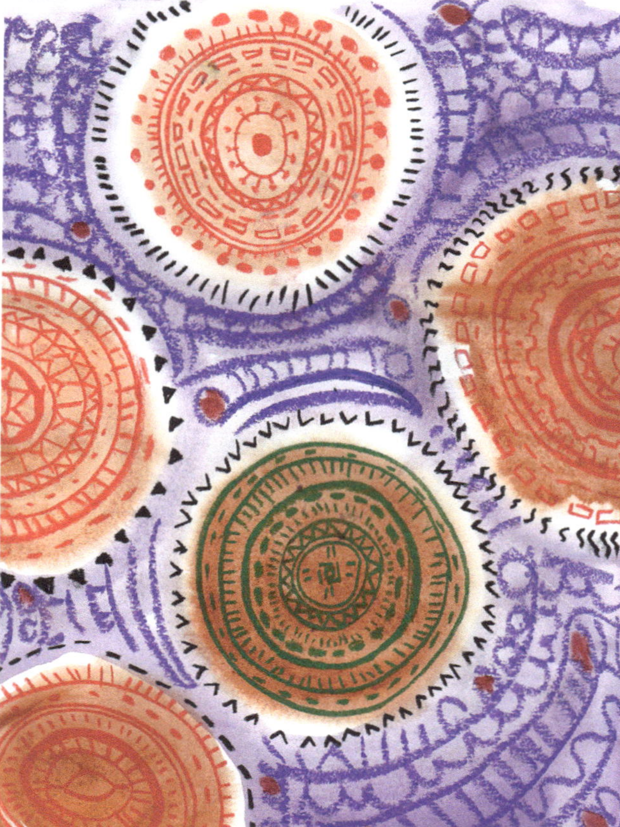
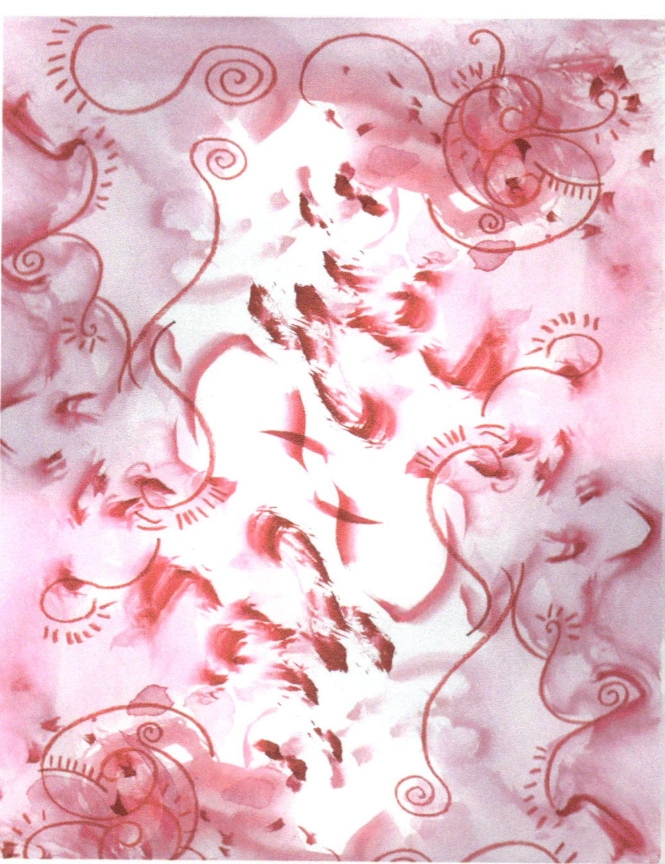

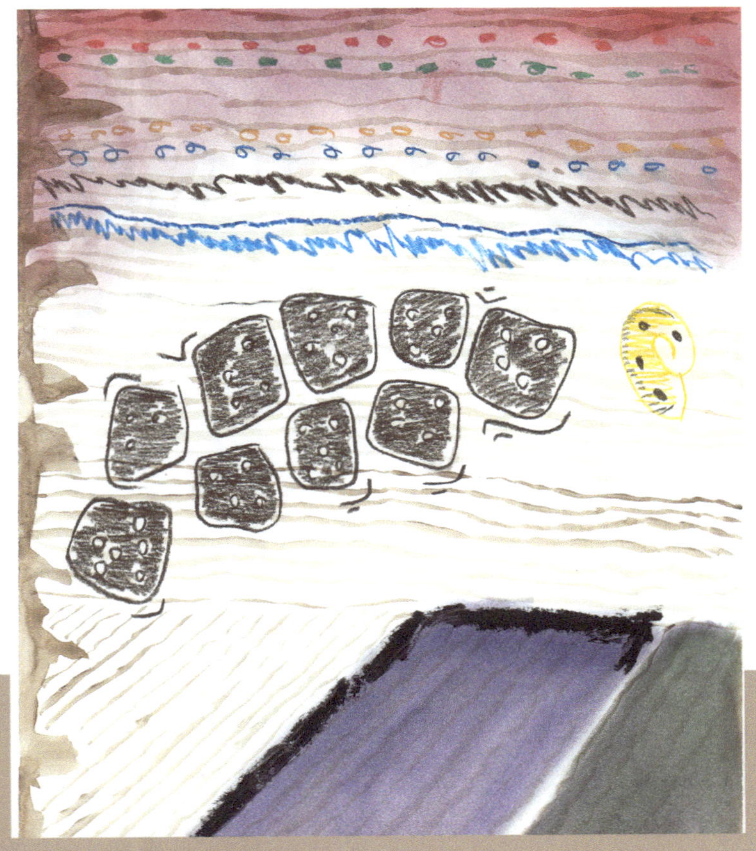

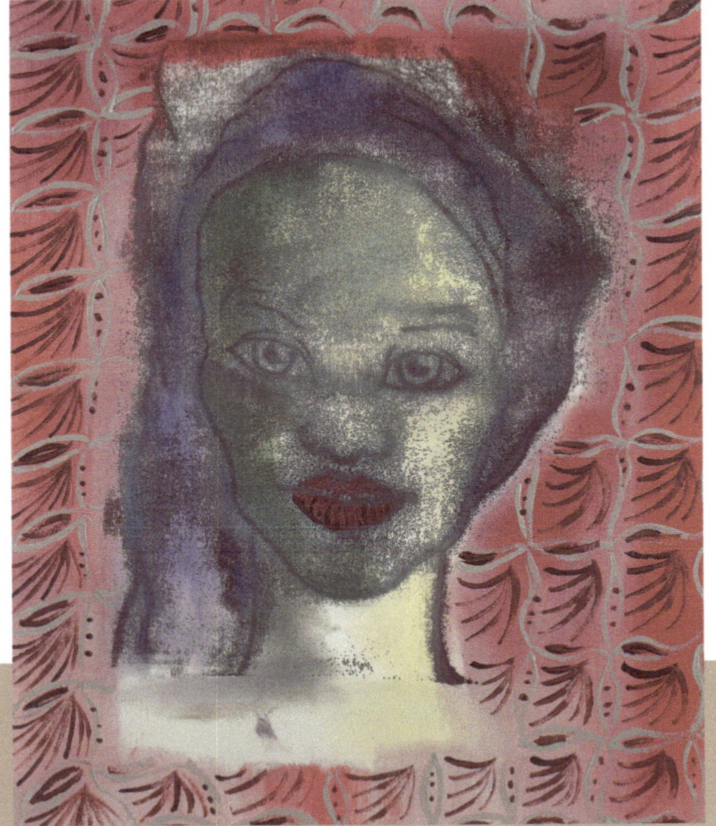

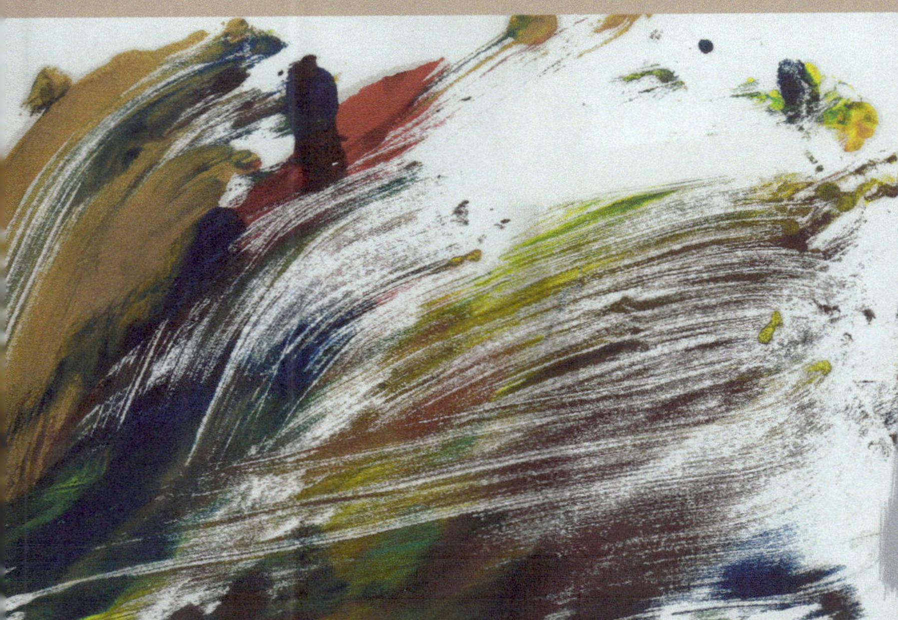

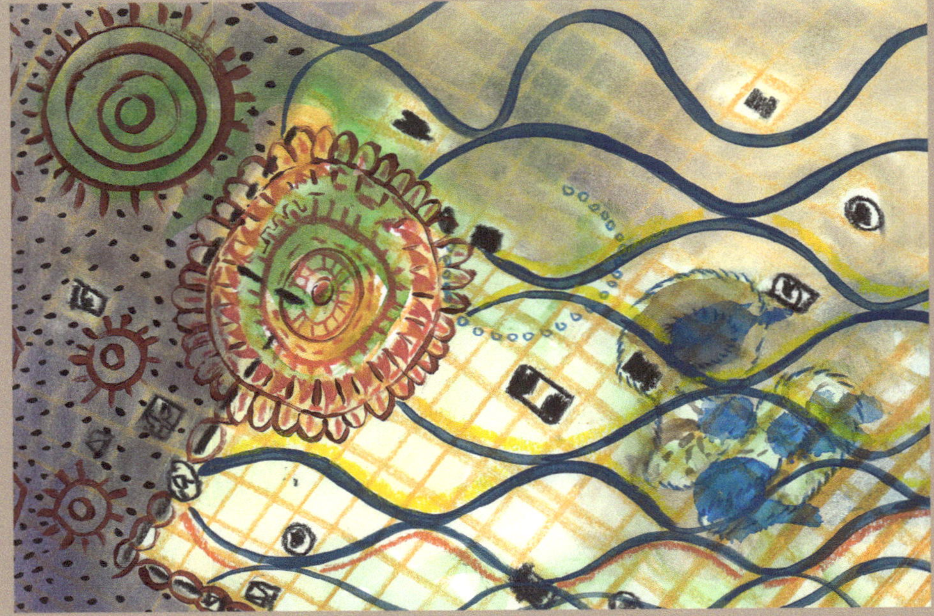

I would say things like, *"You want me to do what now?"* or, *"Just splatter the paint around? Scribble??"* I was totally out of my element… until I wasn't! With her guidance, before I knew it, I was having the time of my life splattering and scribbling and making irregular lines and shapes! With Diane's help, I learned to **explore art styles**, not mindlessly, but instinctively. The way that I had done as a child, long before I learned all of the art principles I'd learned in college. The major difference though, was that now I was able to combine the *sophistication* and *understanding* of making art and apply it from an uninhibited, playful stance.

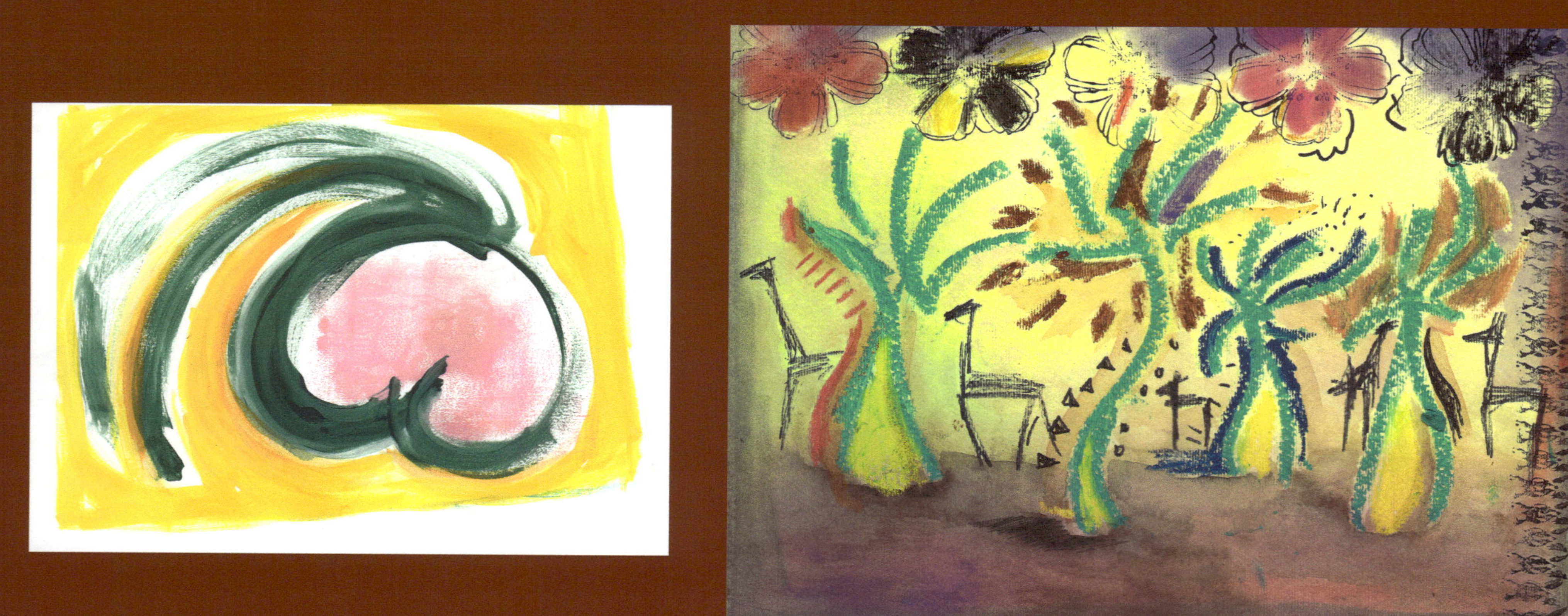

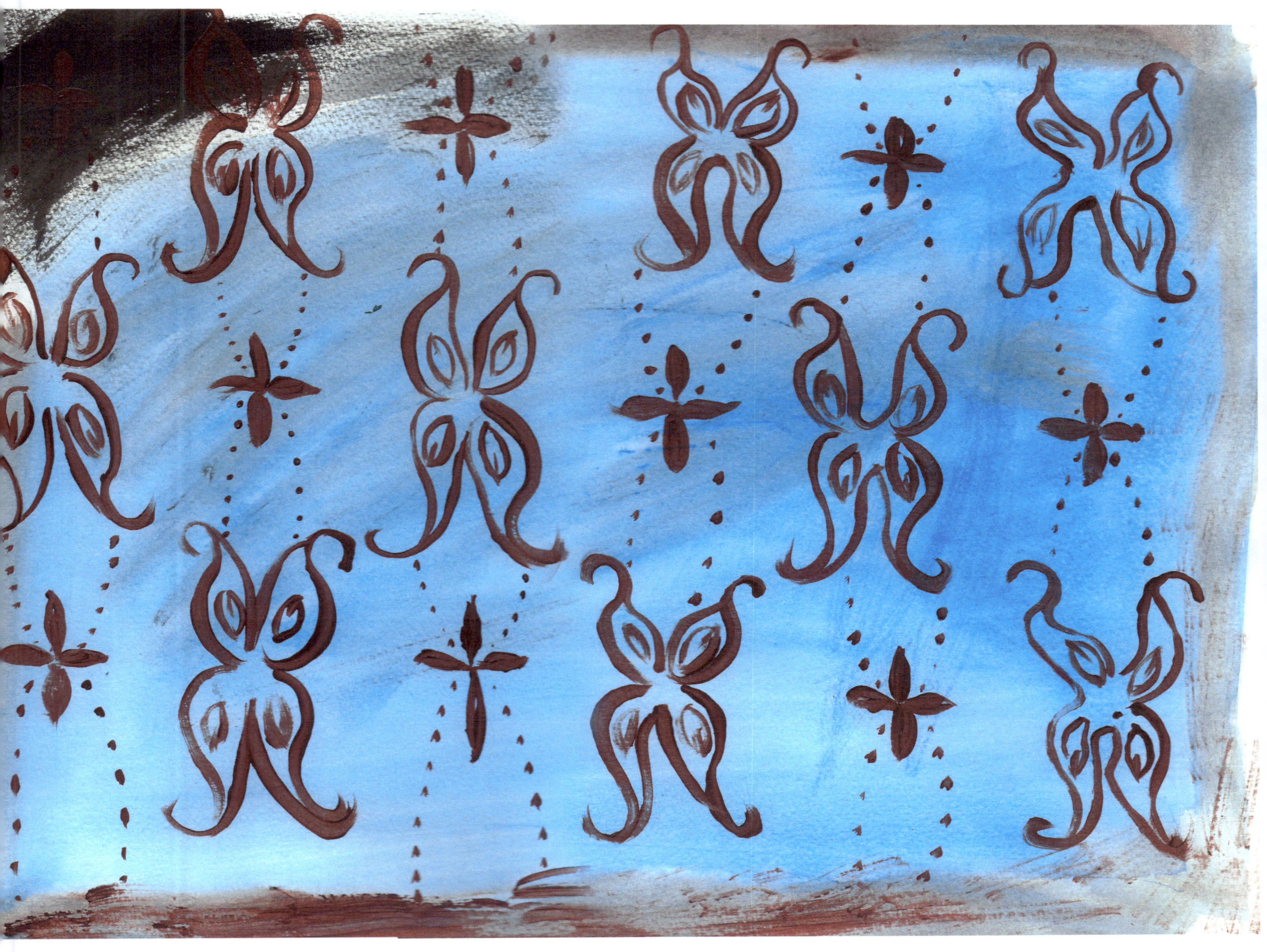

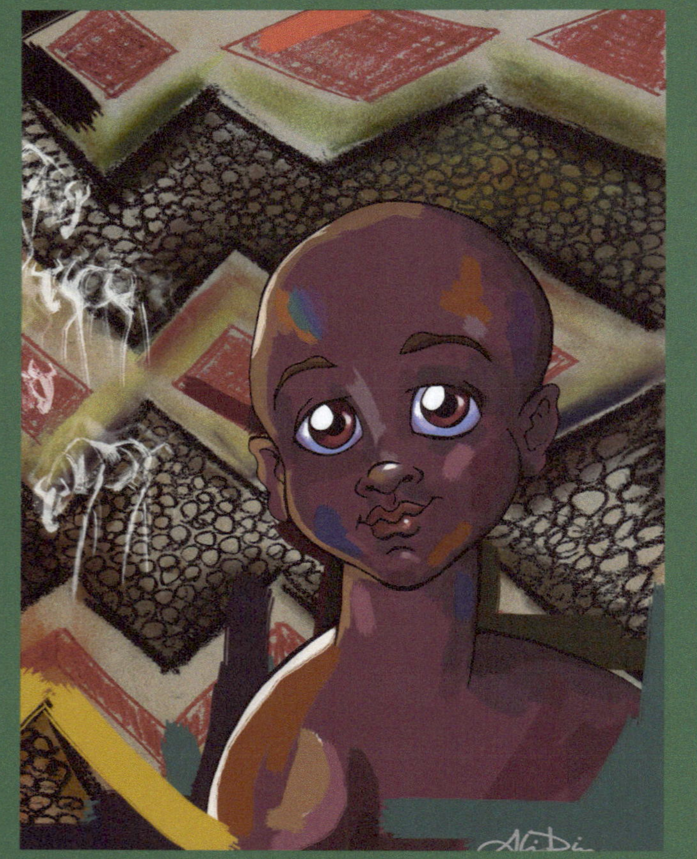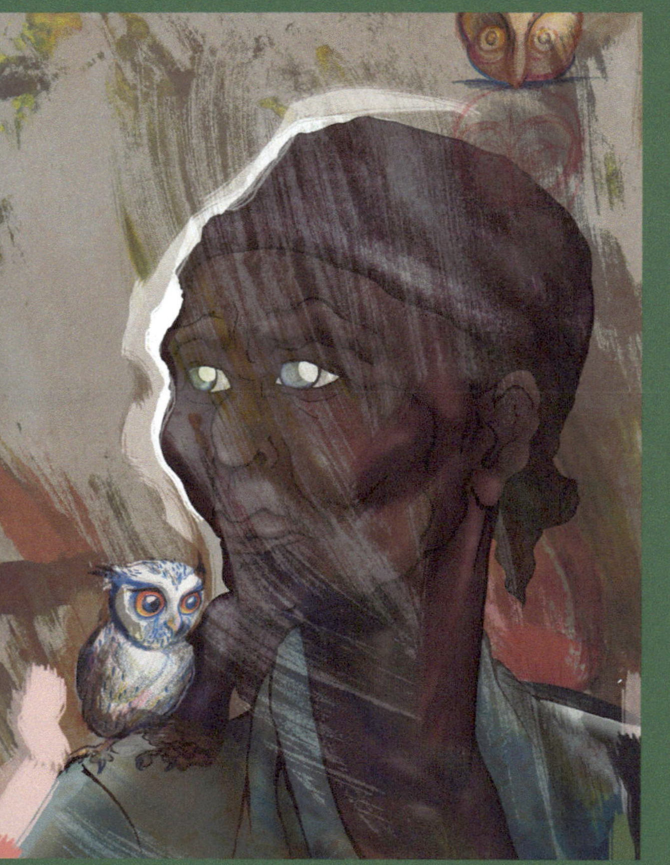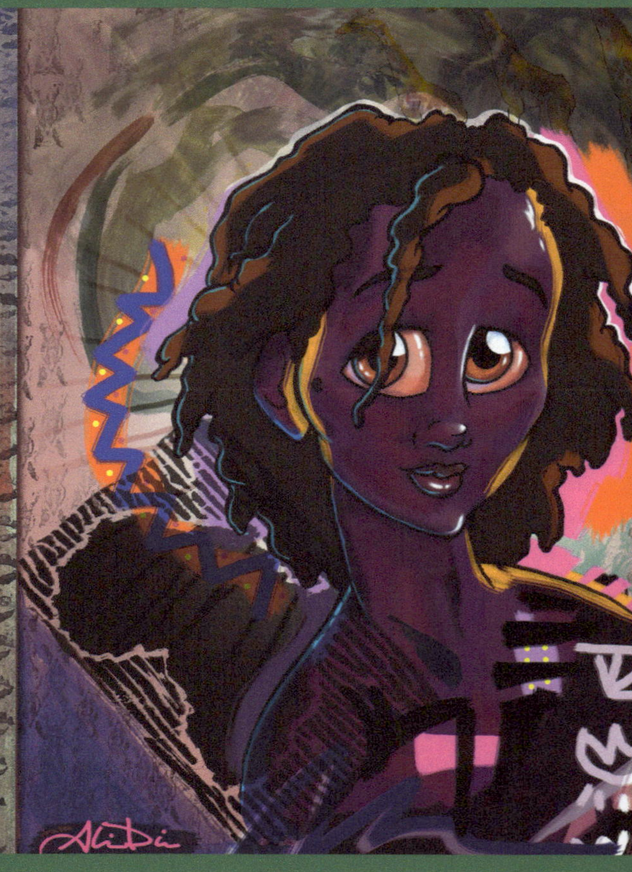

Diane also introduced me to one of my now favorite artists, Jean Michel Basquiat, arguably one of the greatest masters of instinctive, experimental painting to ever live. Through taking this class, I learned to not only listen to my *internal creative voice*, but to *trust* it. This changed the way I would view making art, forever. With my newly acquired skill of experimental painting, and a cast of characters lined up, I began creating my first collection for the *Jaydi's Story* series. I called it *"Inspiration from Kenya."* Probably because it was literally inspired by Kenya. Lol, I know, very profound. It didn't matter, I was developing a visual language for my characters to exist in.

For me, the Mixed Media paintings of this series were how I really got my feet wet and began to bring *Jaydi's Story* to life!

As far as the theme is concerned, I always knew I wasn't creating *Jaydi's Story* for my own benefit. As I've previously mentioned, this project was built out of a dream and the simple act of asking God to *"Use me."* That fact has been the guiding point throughout this entire project. From the time that I had first reached out to the missionaries in Albuquerque, I had the same looming question in my head, *"How can I help?"* The answer came, I first needed to learn more. To learn more, I began asking more questions, deeper questions. Questions such as how finances were used in the organization to benefit the needs of the people… although uncomfortable, this allowed my thought process to expand.

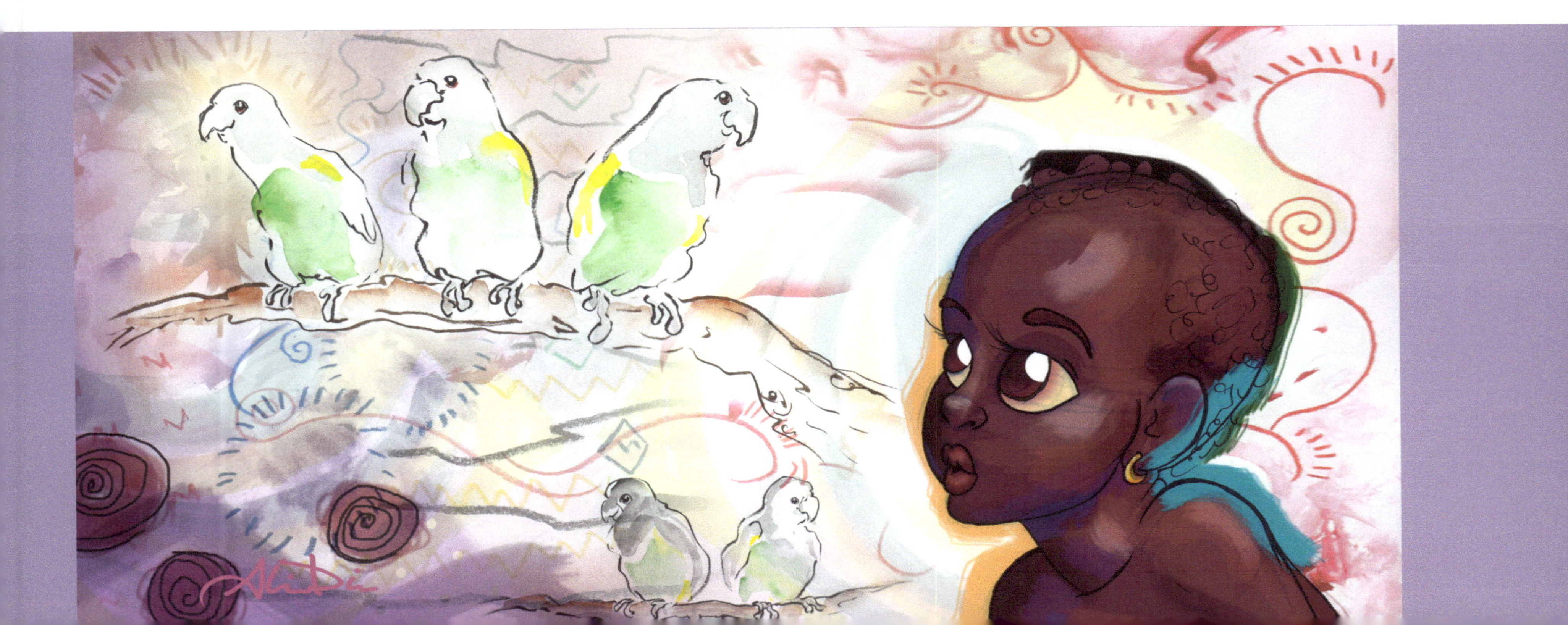

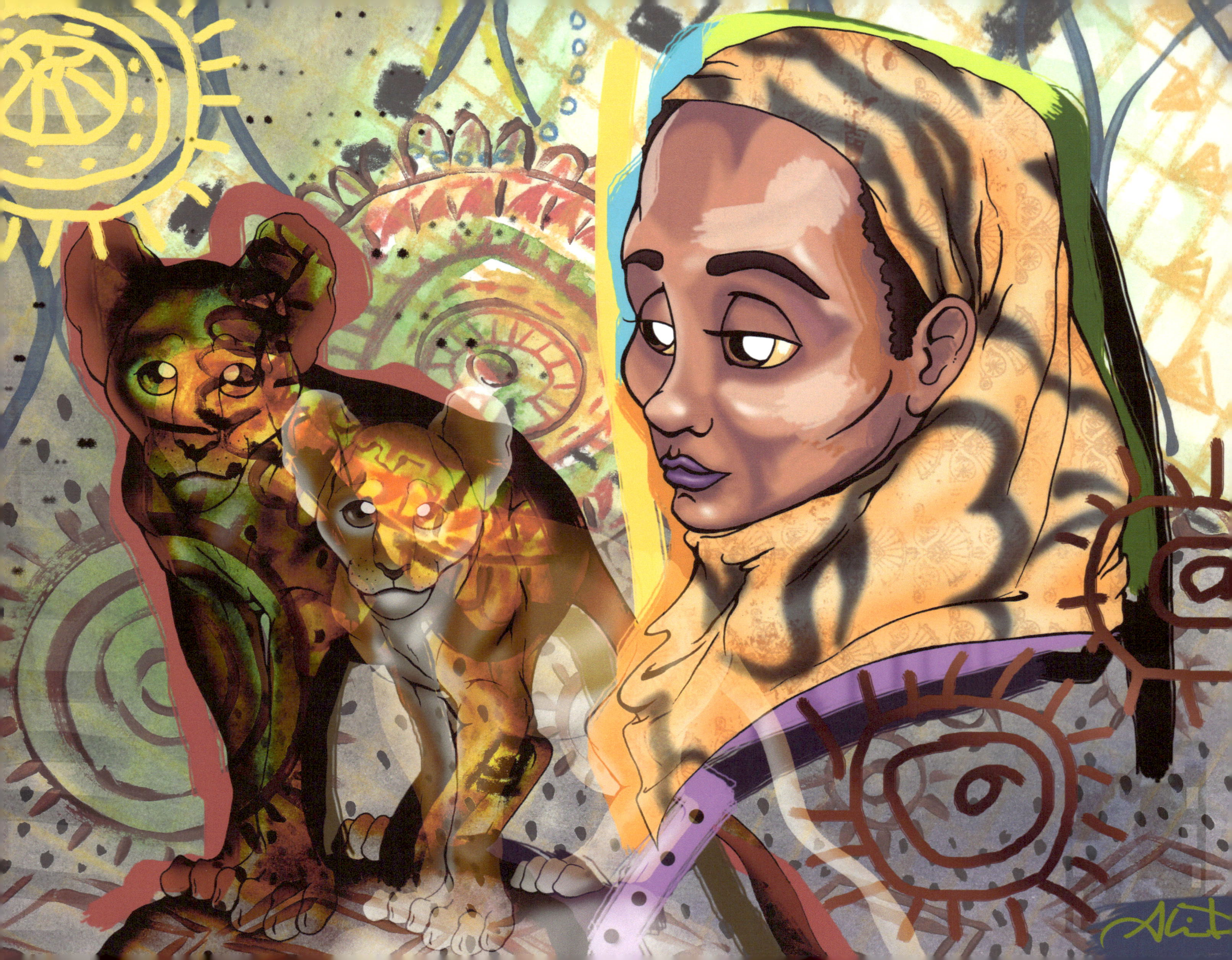

I brainstormed ways I could contribute. From there, I came up with my first plan, which was to donate 30% of proceeds from the *"Inspiration from Kenya"* collection to support the missionary efforts in Kwale.

Eventually, I would find other organizations who were also doing good works in Kenya, which allowed me to expand into other regions I could reach as well, such as Nairobi and Chwele. Through this exploration and discovery of purpose, I was able to **uncover a theme.** *Jaydi's Story* would exist to contribute to improving the lives for girls in Kenya.

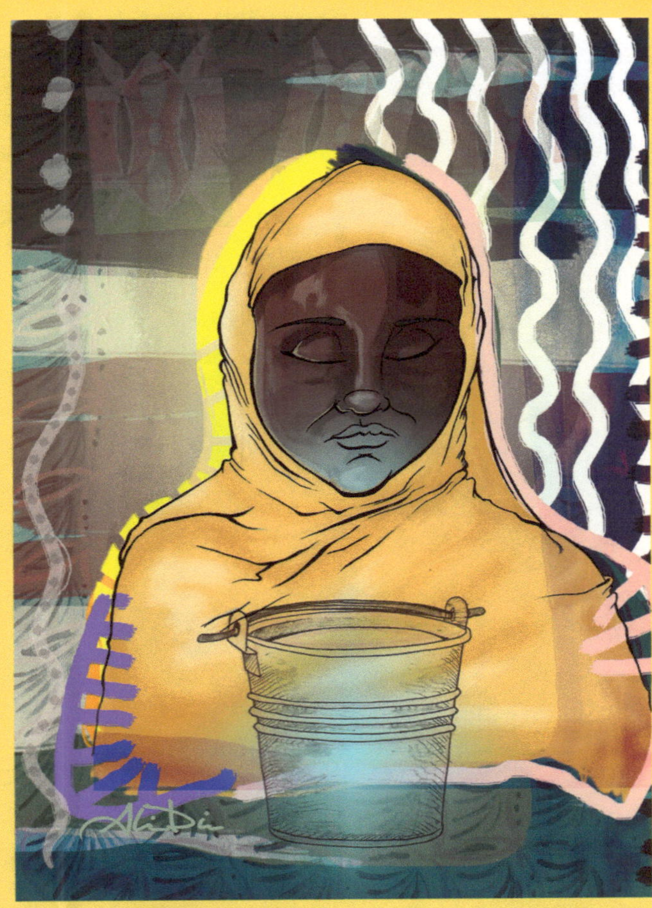

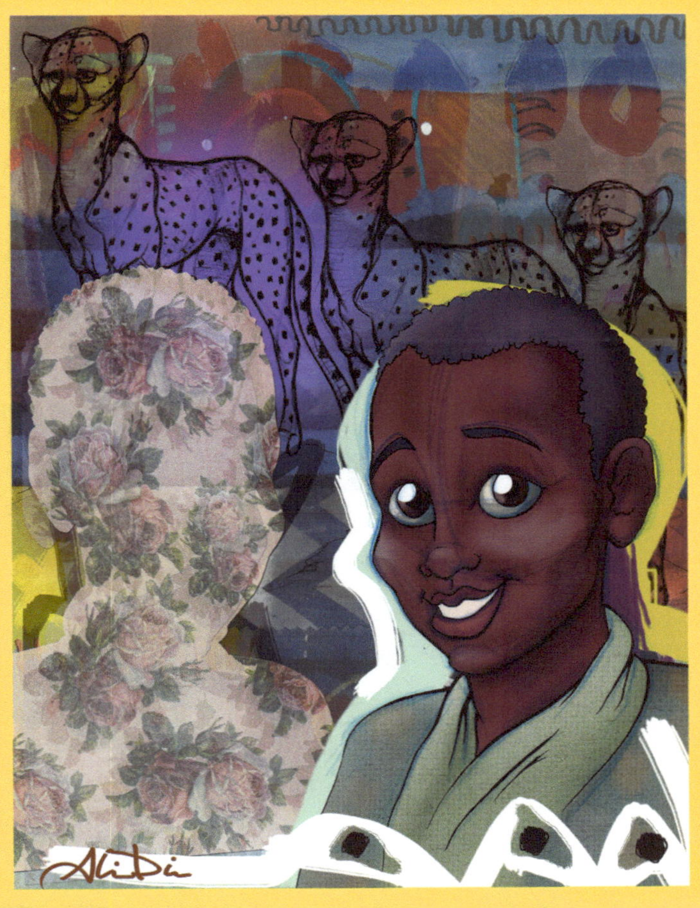

Explore Art Styles & Uncover a Theme: Reflection Questions

1. What artists can you learn from to get you out of your *creative comfort zone?*
2. What classes might you take or books might you read on an art technique you've never tried before? Take a free or inexpensive course in that technique.
3. What artists *inspire* you? What colors do they use? *Textures? Mediums? Subject matter?*
4. Based on your *Inspiration* (from **Step 1**), what recurring question(s) come up for you?
5. Is there a *greater cause* that your project can serve? Write it down and find 2-3 organizations currently involved in this mission.

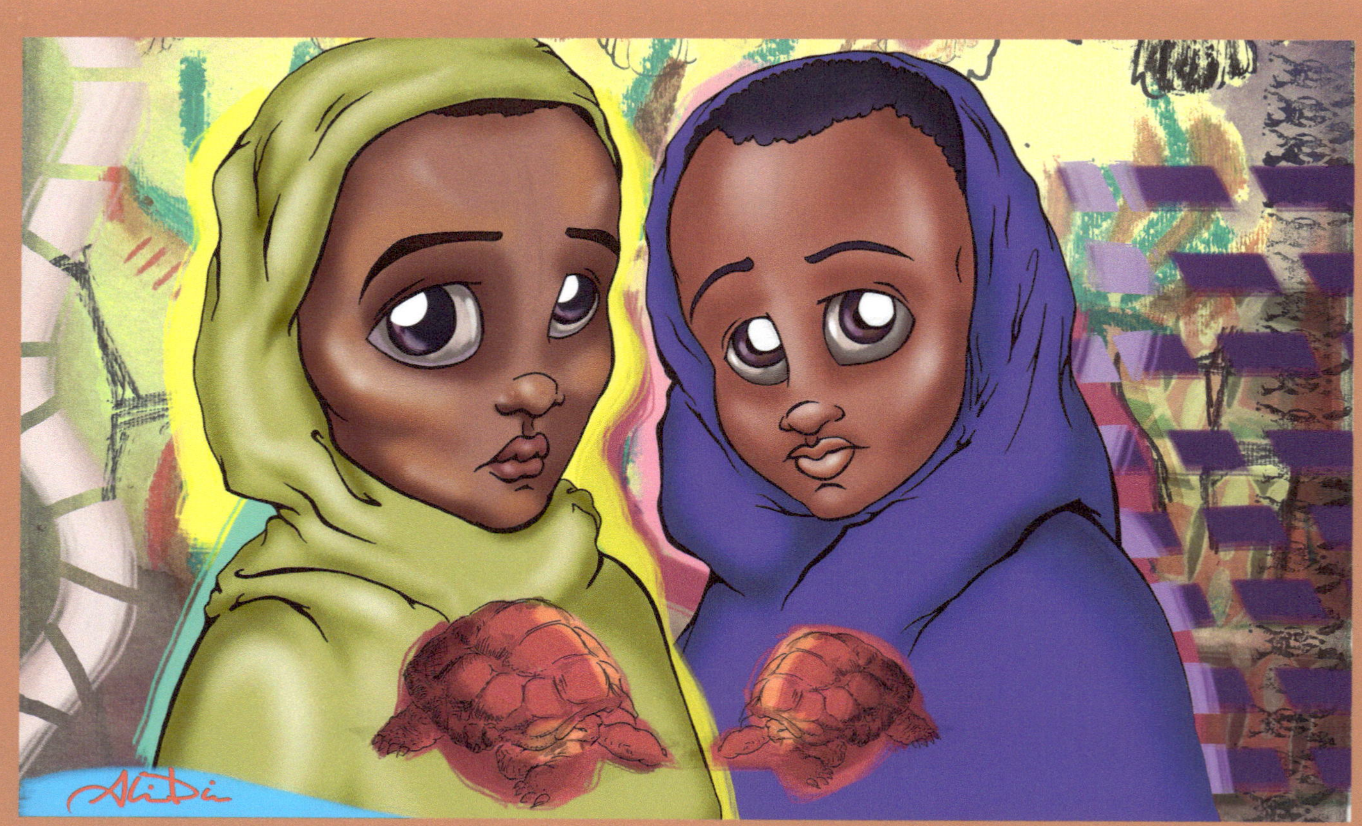

Step 4: Research & Create a World

Do you remember that scene in Pixar's *Soul,* when the character, *Twenty-Two,* is trying to find her inspiration? Being led through the *Hall of Everything, Joe Gardner* helps *Twenty-Two* try a variety of possible professions which could be her passion in life, her *"spark."* One of the professions she tries is Art, in which she immediately gives up, insisting that *"Hands are hard!"* Which, if you are an visual artist, you probably know that drawing hands is one of the most challenging drawing subjects to master! I say all this say, *"Studying history is hard!"* Or more specifically, *"Studying **African** History is hard! Real hard!"* However, it was a vital step for me in the first phase of creating a world, which is **research!**

Research for me, was to begin the process of learning *the good, the bad* and the *everything in-between* of African History. And, yes! It was indeed difficult, because once I made it past the inevitable horrors of the Trans-Atlantic slave trade (and learning what actually was and wasn't even true regarding said slave trade) there was a world of *Colonization* for me to discover… which in a word, is just downright, depressing. Some things, though, are worth sludging through the mud to get to the proverbial *Blood Diamonds* of enlightenment waiting on the other side!

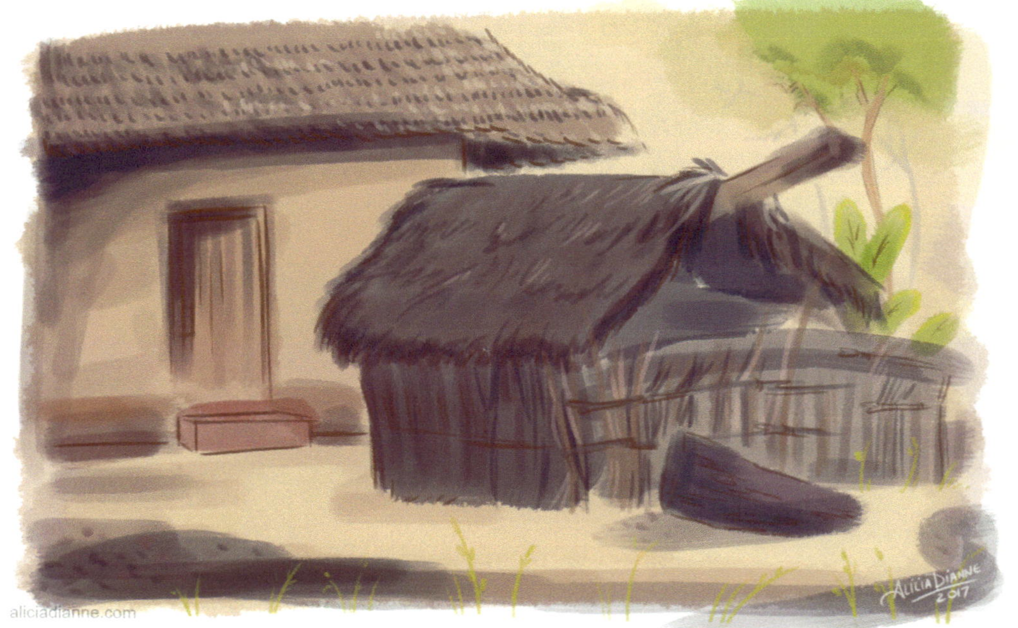

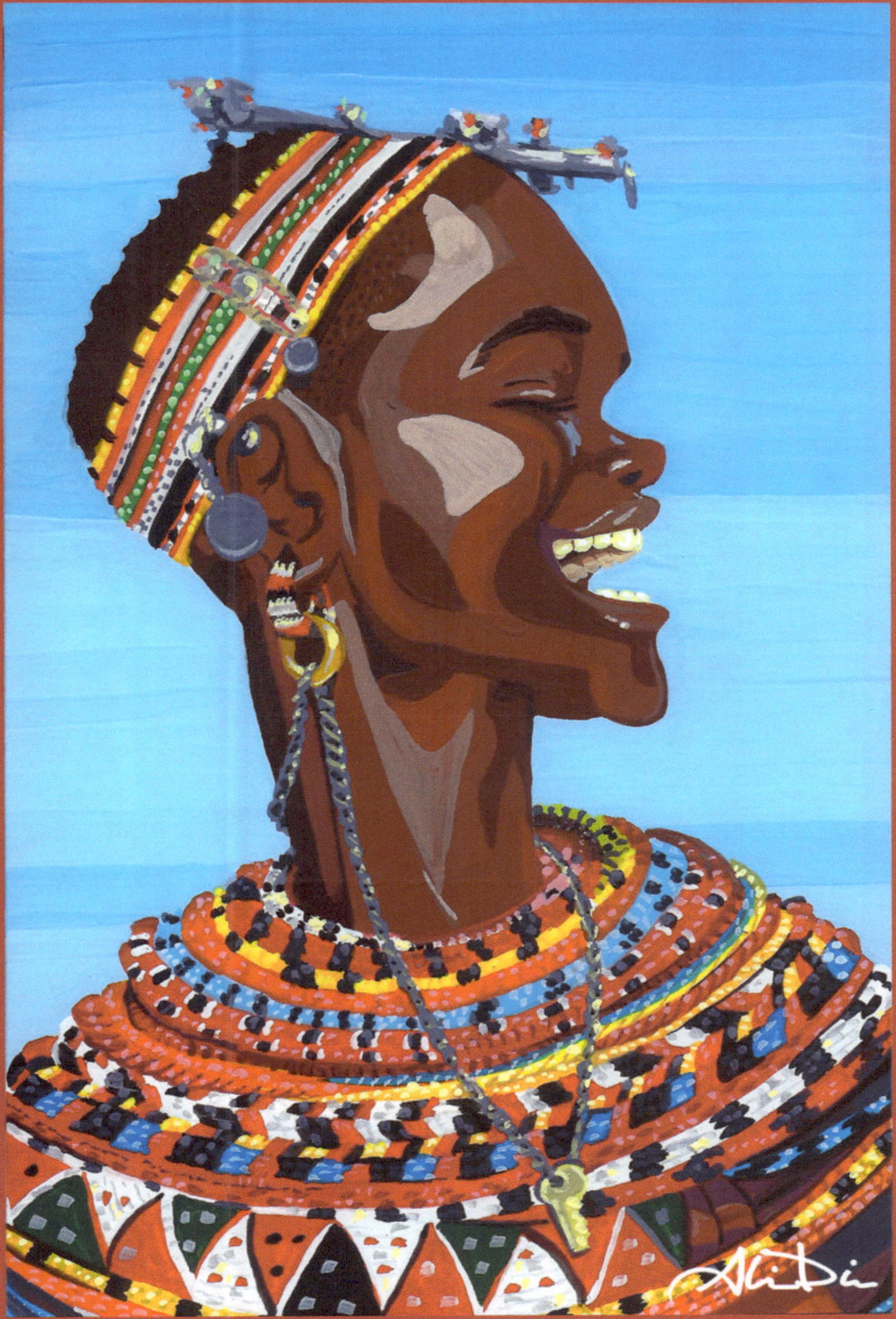

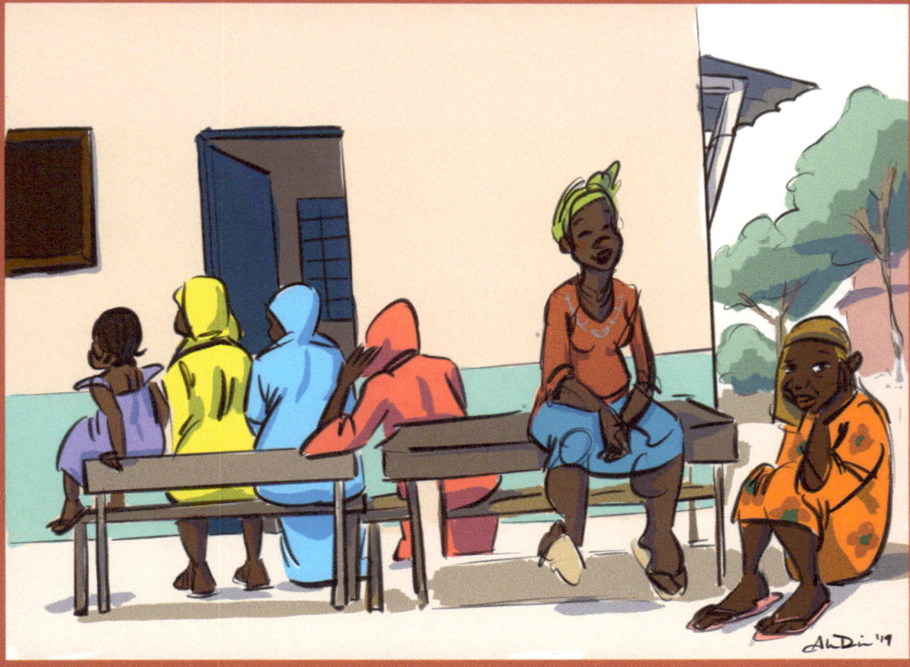

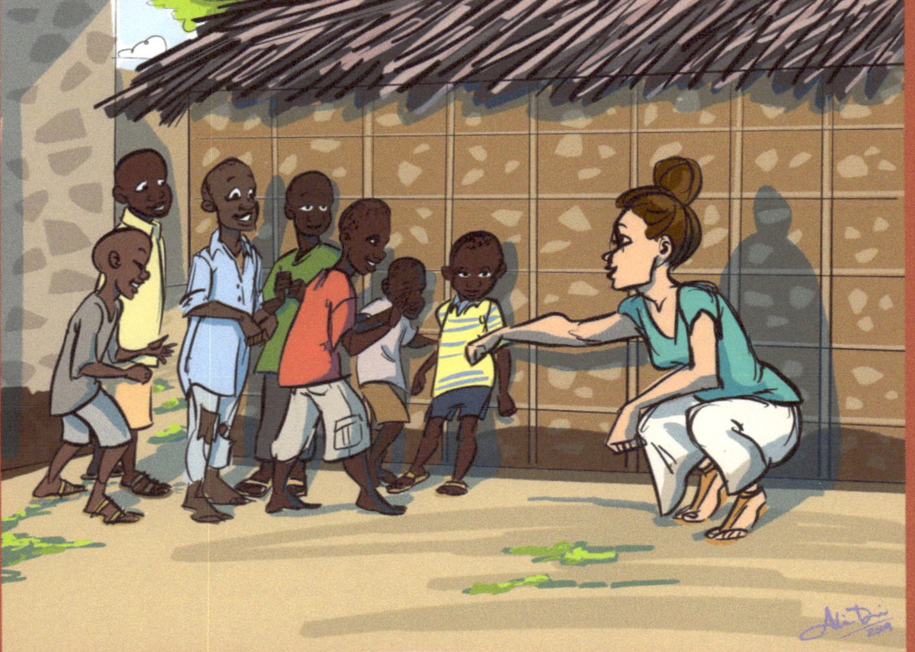

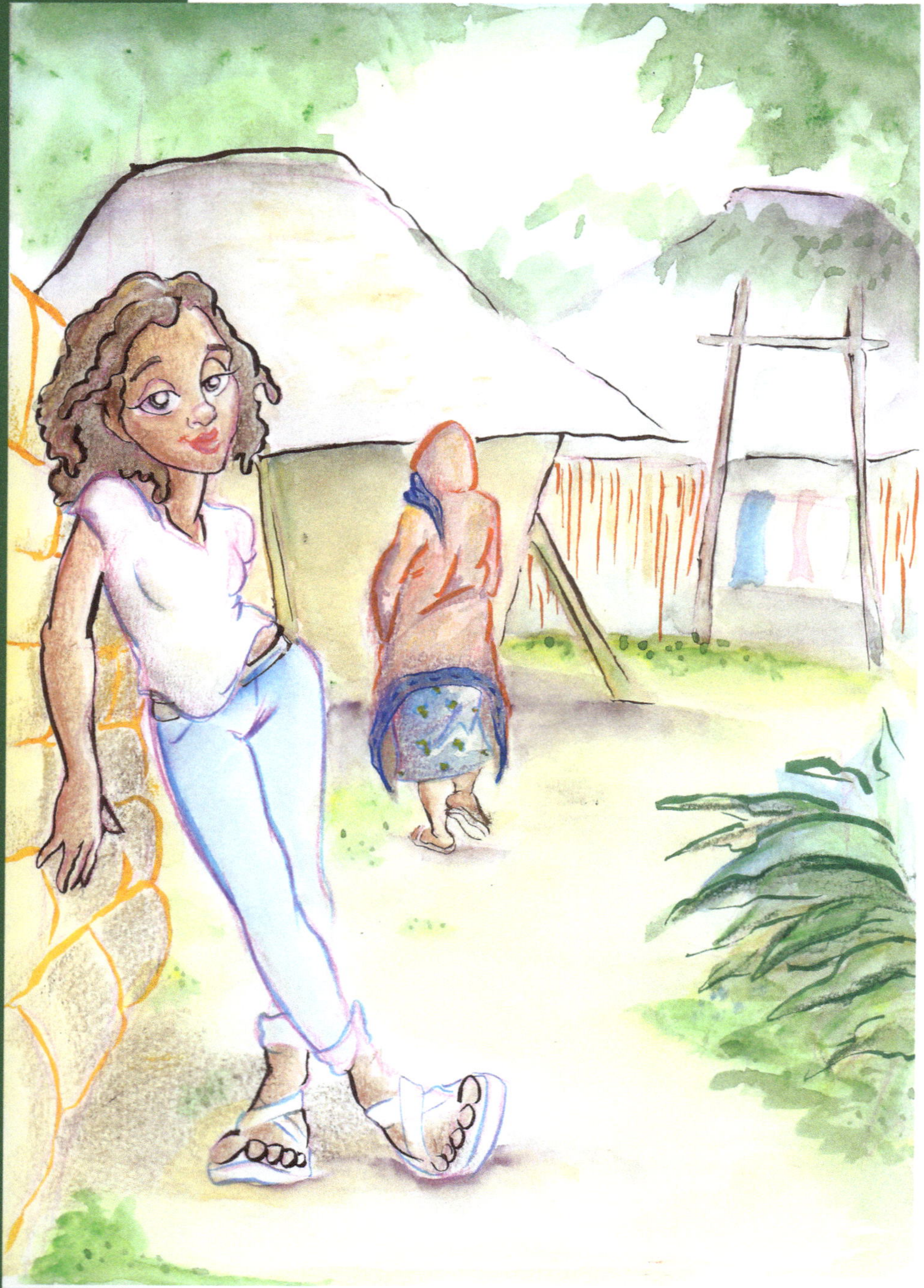

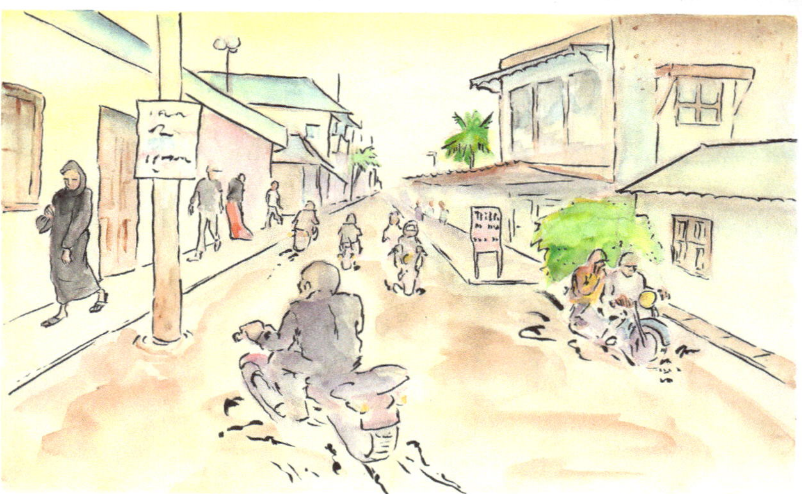

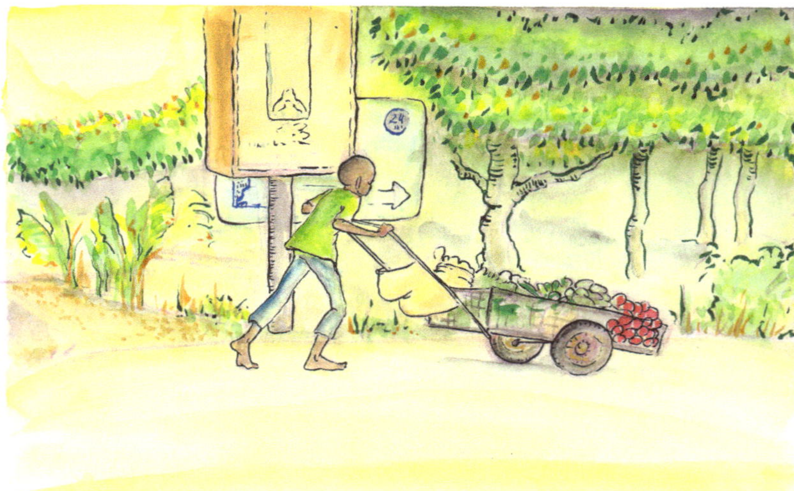

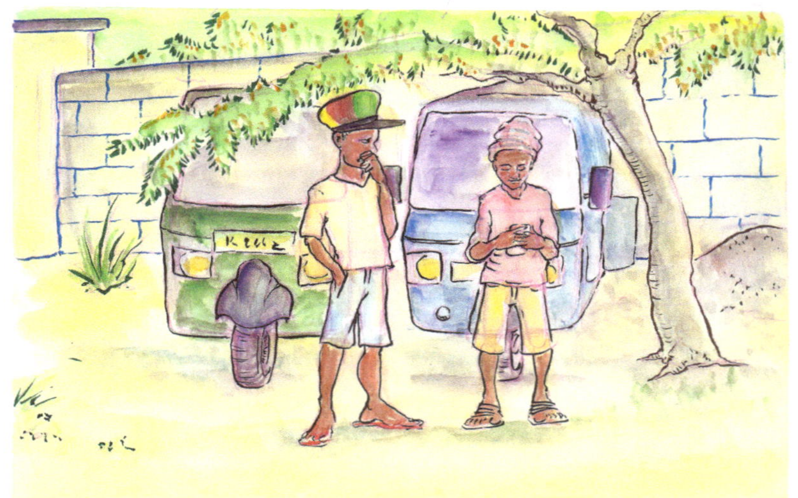

"Inspiration from Kenya" Watercolors

Let me tell you, once you get a little dirty and begin to discover the history of your own ancestry, the experience can be described in only one word, *liberating!* The process of that journey can be found in my articles, *Discovering African History*, and *Discovery African Identity*.

What I also began researching, which is not included in my articles, is discovering African *Folklore*. This part of research was actually really fun! Fairytales, as I've discovered, are not inherently out of Europe, as commonly thought of today. In fact, if you do a little digging, you may find that *every* culture has there own myths, legends, superstitions, monsters, magic and mischief-makers. Many of these stories are creation stories, and many others, such as *Aesop's Fables*, are used to teach children (and perhaps us all) a valuable lesson. As is evident in perhaps the most famous of African Folktales, *The Tortoise and the Hare*. So much of *Jaydi's* **Story** is inspired by just that, *stories*. A mass collective of cultural stories I read about from all over the continent.

I've credited Diane with my discovery of Experimental Painting. I now must pay homage to another of my great mentors, Deborah Ross. For if it were not for Deborah's devout passion for watercolor, I might have never discovered my absolute love of the medium. Deborah is a one of a kind, just one of those truly special and entirely distinct humans you only meet once in a lifetime. She is to me, the "Jane Goodall" of painting, for she has devoted her career to painting wildlife, which she does on-site. She has spent decades making extensive trips to several African countries, including Kenya, both making and teaching art. She captures her images of nature using only one medium, watercolor.

As my professor at the School of Visual Arts from Freshman to Junior year, I studied both Figure Drawing and Wildlife Drawing under her watchful eye. With her persistence, I learned very slowly, to grow comfortable with the world's fussiest medium.

Watercolor, if you are not familiar, is very unforgiving. It can't be covered over like other paint and it can't be meddled with, as doing so will entirely destroy both the image and the paper. Watercolor requires very specific paper weights (thickness), as well as textures. It has a mind of its own! If you refuse to learn the way the medium *thinks*, it will completely rebel against you instead of working with you! And you try to control it, it will revolt.

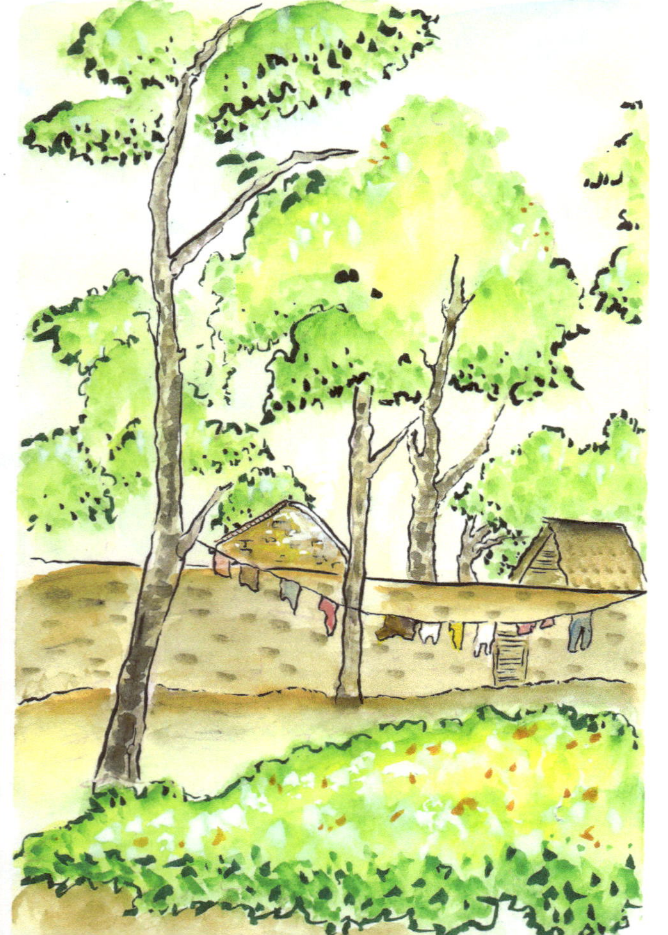
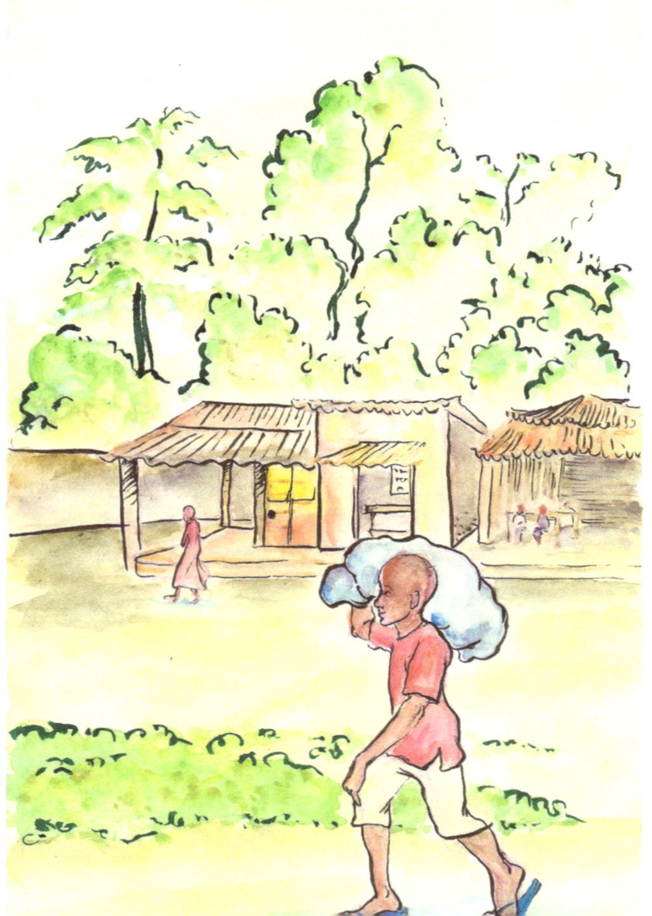
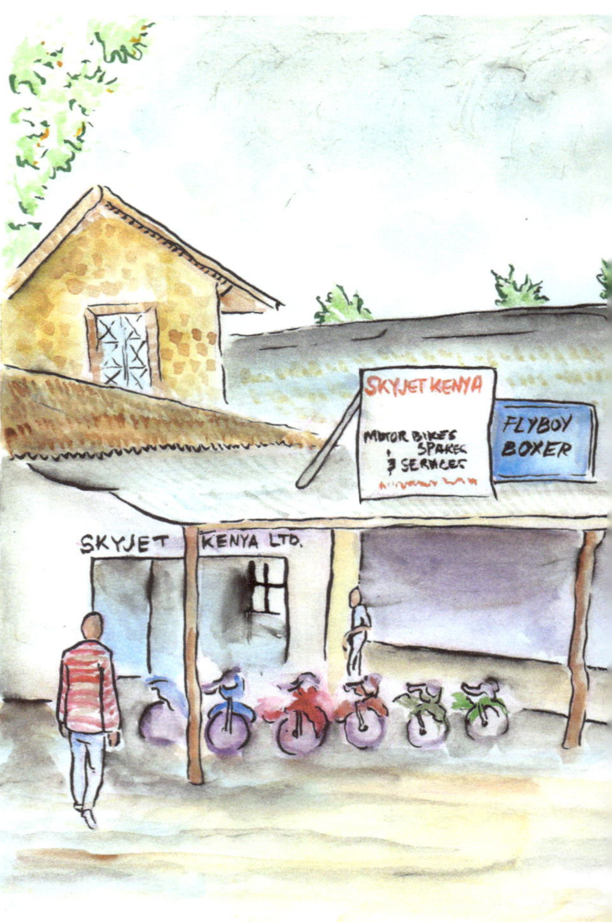

For one to really work with watercolor, the artist must first learn to *respect* it. They must learn its, dare I say, *personality?* One must work in harmony with it, only then can you truly create something special! Then the watercolor will dance harmoniously *with* you,

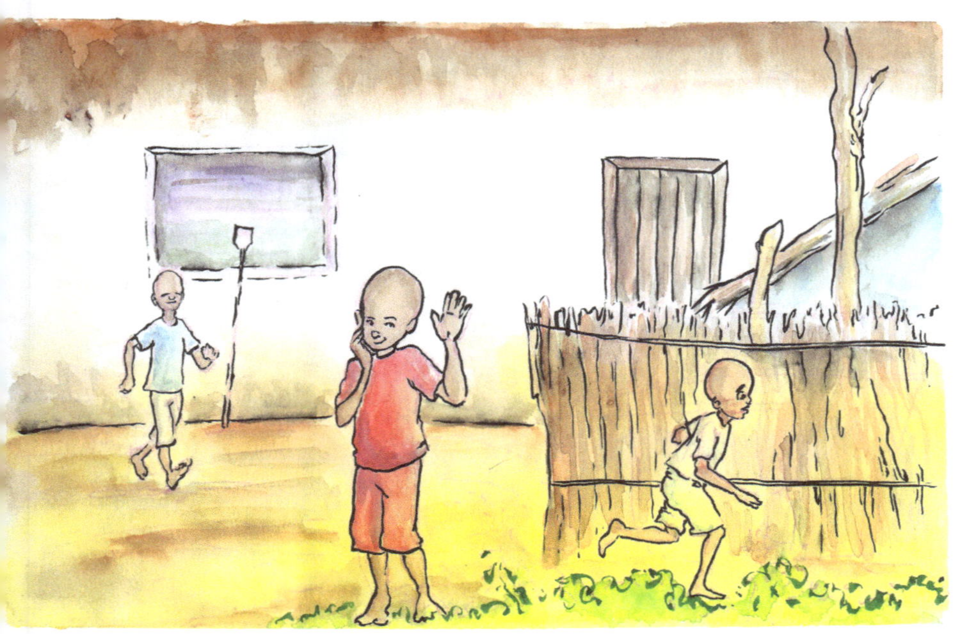

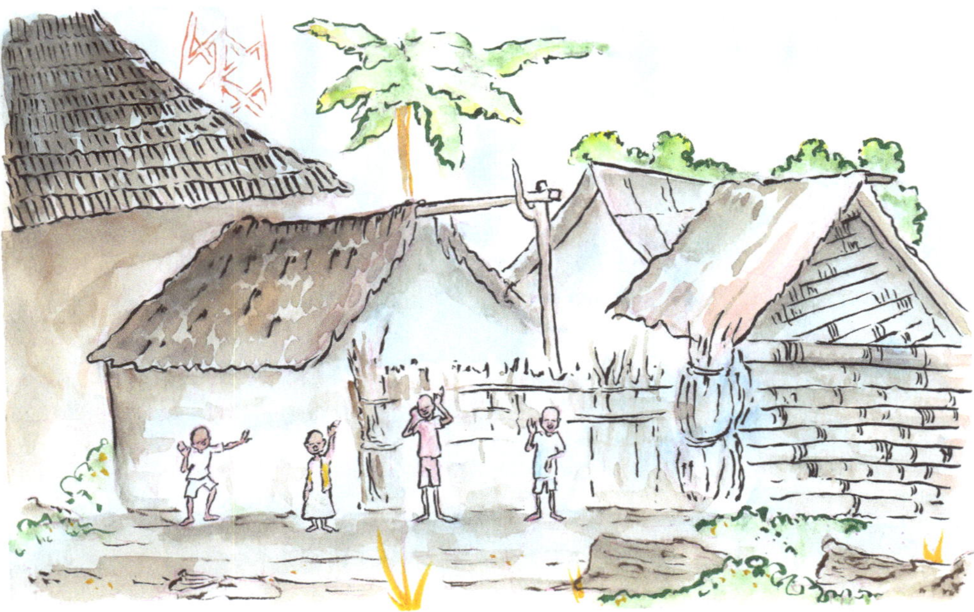

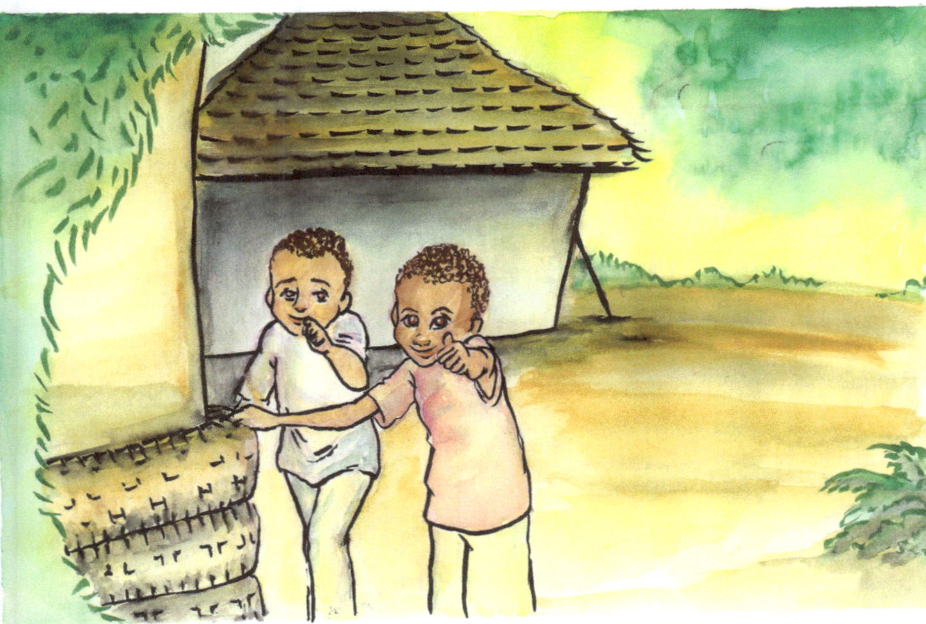

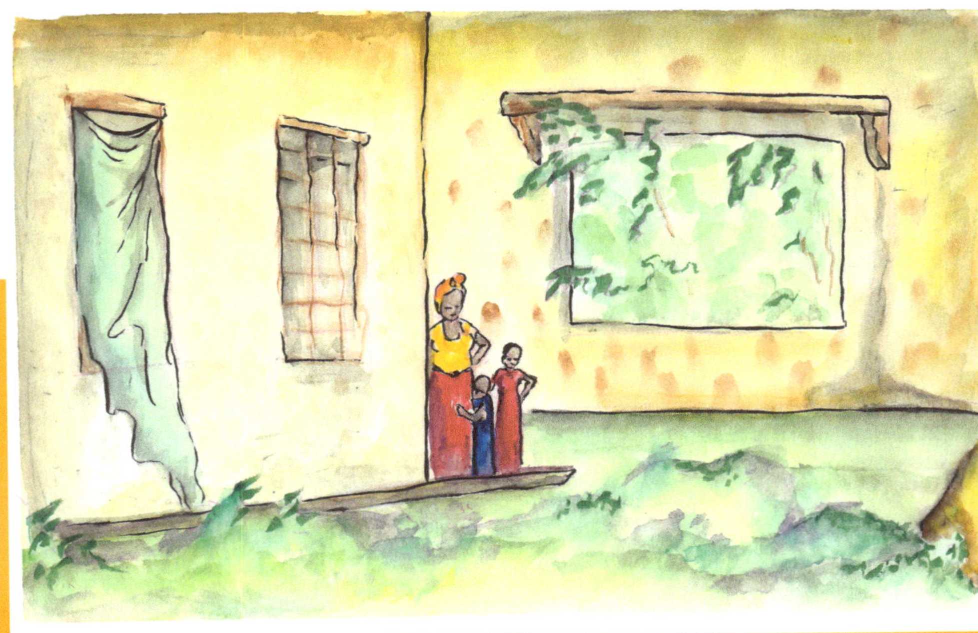

but never for you! I say all of this to say, through the learning of the use of watercolor, I was able to uncover the *moods* it can bring to a work. The mood is truly what you want to uncover during this next stage of your process.

This process became vital to **create a world** for *Jaydi's Story*. After all, my character's would need someplace to live, wouldn't they? As I have learned from talking to some of the best concept artists in the Animation industry, *"You don't get good at creating backgrounds, until you understand that the background is **also** a character!"*

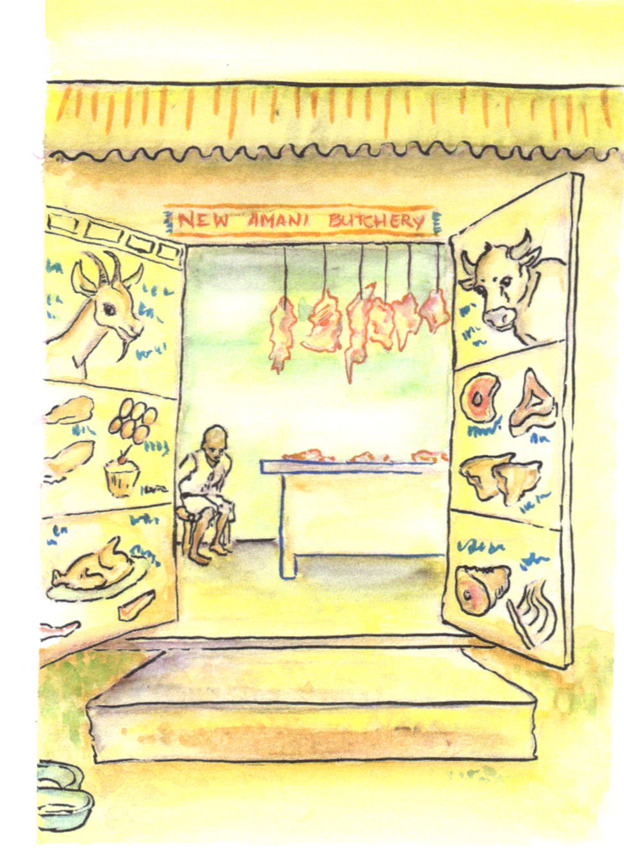

At this point, creating your world will be a process of building an atmosphere, evoking emotion through your choice of color, style, texture and light, *as well as* determining the laws of what does or does not exist in this space. In order to build the world of *Jaydi's Story*, I began creating a series of moody environments, which would exist essentially as characters themselves! As I searched deeply

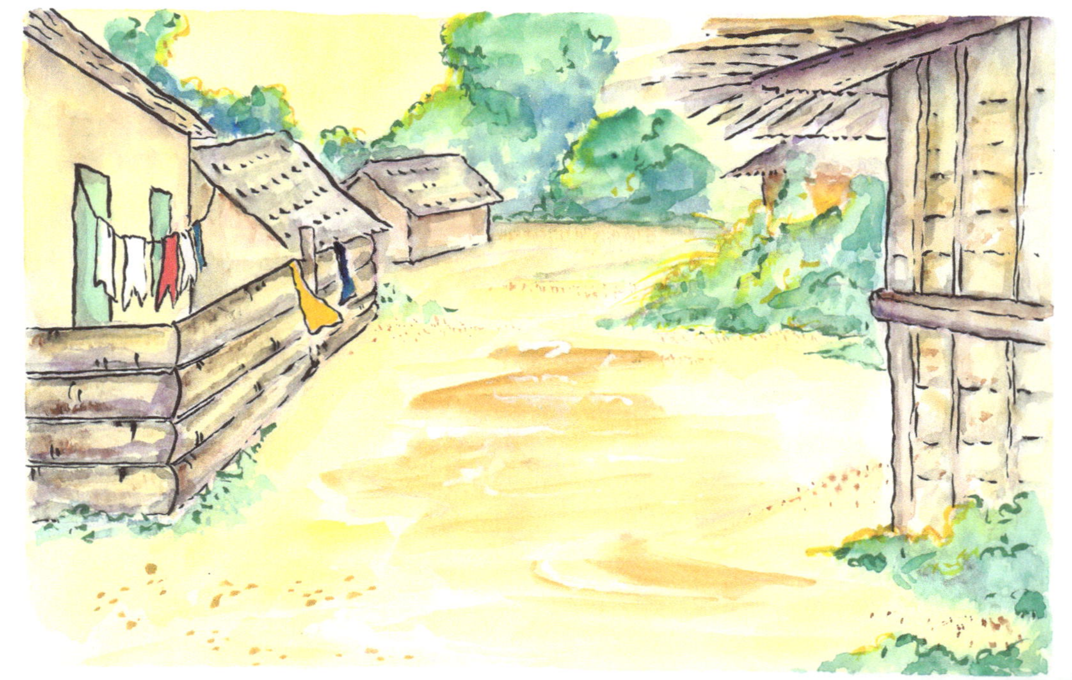

into the atmosphere of these settings, I considered details such as the weather, fabric patterns, cultural dynamics, modes of transportation, and even, the presence of the supernatural. I used references and created a *mood board* - a collection of inspirational images and references put together on a board to refer to. Over time, I created multiple mood boards, physical and digital. Slowly, this process began to reveal a world through which my characters could exist. The series of explorative watercolor paintings I created in this process would eventually become *Jaydi's* world, they would become *Kaweria Township*.

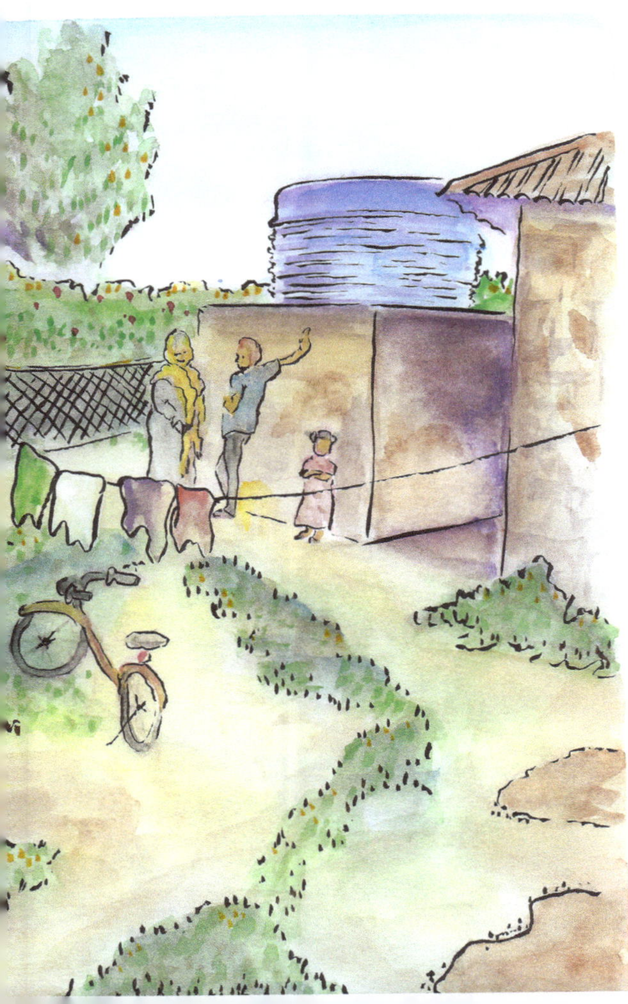
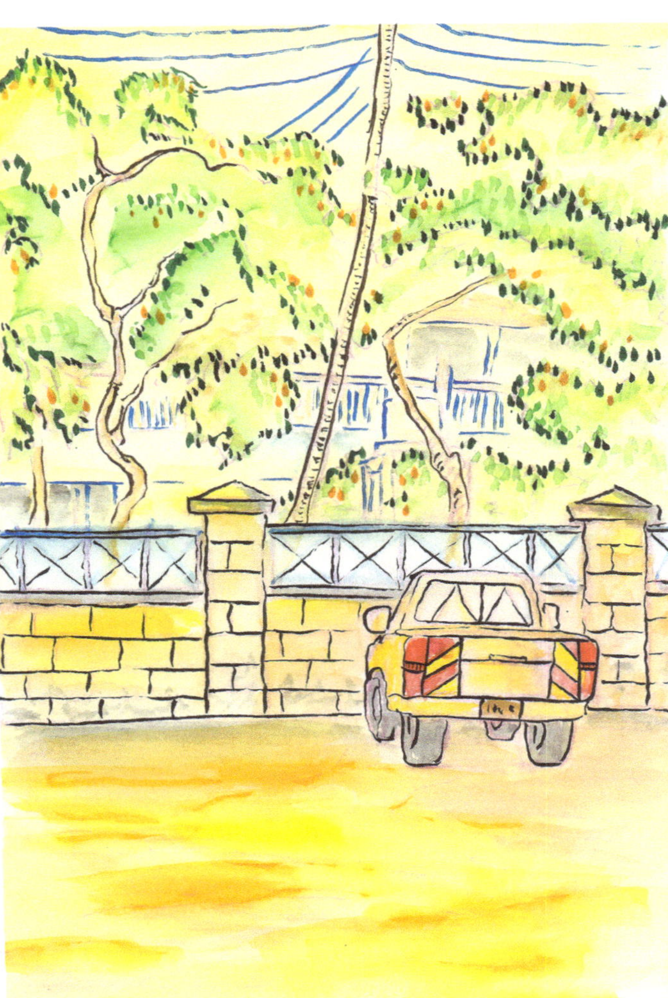
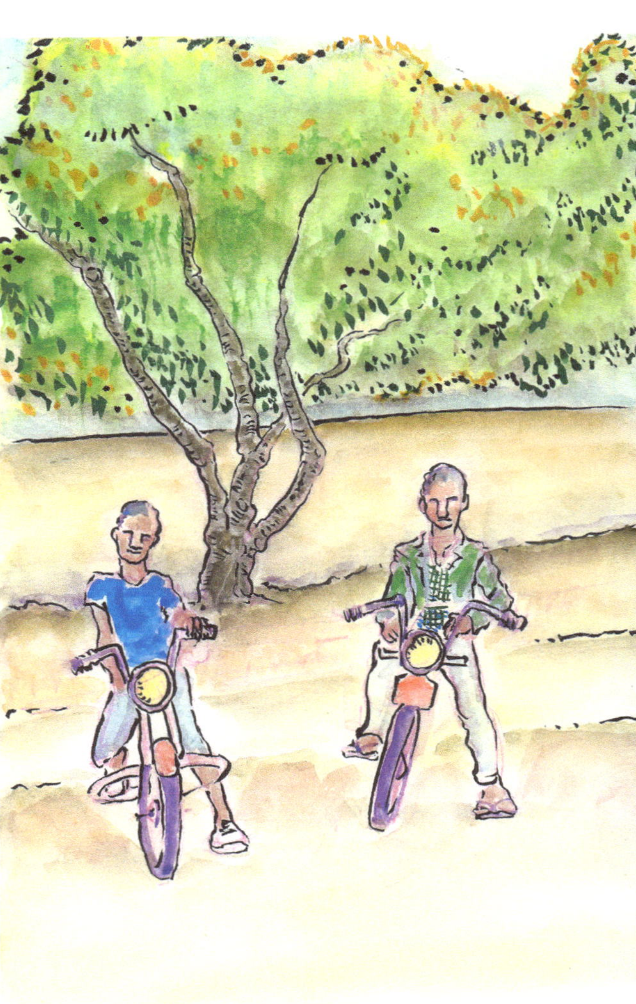

Research & Create a World: Reflection Questions

1. What cultural histories are inspiring you? What can you do to learn more about them?
2. What folktales, myths or legends come from your own continent or country of origin?
3. What mediums do you enjoy woking with and will keep you motivated?
4. Decide what real location(s) your world is based on and determine what natural and supernatural laws exist within it.
5. Create a *Mood Board* of inspirational images to inspire you. Get mood board ideas in the **Resource List** in the back of this book
6. Create a variety of 8-10 artworks which represent the location, time period and tone you would like your characters to exist in.

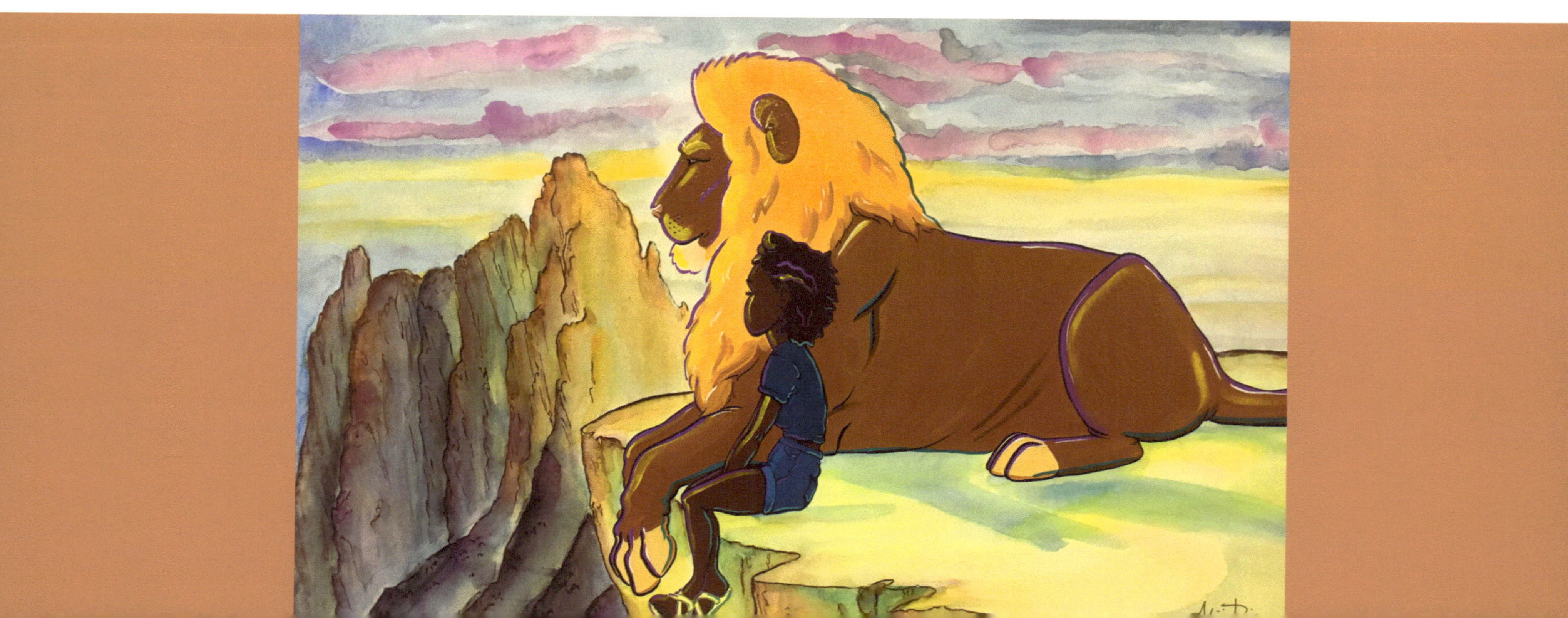

Step 5: Maintain Momentum

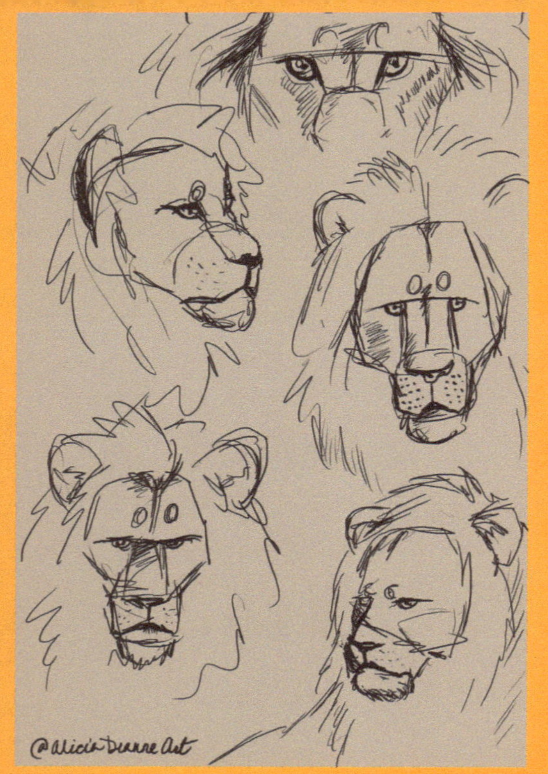

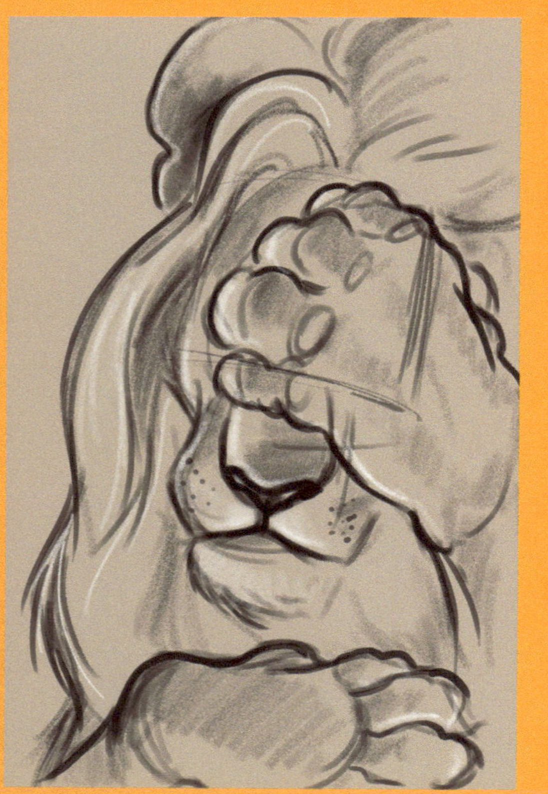

After every high there is a low, as they say. I certainly was not without either in my process. So once I had my characters and I had their environment, I fell into a creative slump. I wasn't sure what to do. I felt completely inadequate to write, and thought *"maybe someday"* I can find a writer… from Kenya… who is no doubt, more worthy to create the story. Even though I knew that I had been given the very roots of this story in my own dream, where I had *seen* the main character.

Although by this time I had been inspired, I still wasn't confident enough in my own writing to do it myself. So I came up with another idea, to do something that I did feel confident in, *make more drawings!* I decided to create a collection of drawings of an animal that I'd felt connected to for years. The Lion. I began working on a project I called *1,000 Lions for Kenya*, which I began as a precursor to *Jaydi's Story*. Some may call this procrastination (and believe me, my story *does* involve procrastination) but this wasn't it! This warm up was my best effort to **maintain momentum** for *Jaydi's Story* while I was waiting for the next stage of development to ripen. It was a place holder, and this little place holder of mine involved literally *hundreds* of drawings, illustrations and character designs - from loose and sketchy to fully rendered - which became a light for me get inspired by, explore, and get my creative juices flowing in a time when I might've otherwise, given up. What, might you think, was happening to my drawing ability during this time? If you guessed, *getting better*, you're absolutely correct! I describe my inspiration for choosing the iconic "lion," as well as my history with them in my upcoming book, *1,000 Lions for Kenya*.

For the next 2 years I would continue to work on drawings and paintings for *1,000 Lions*. Yet, I also wanted to get comfortable telling stories again. I had gotten some of my first formal training in storytelling while studying Animation (which is really, all about story). During this time, at the School of Visual Arts (SVA), I would write and animate stories and characters for my short films.

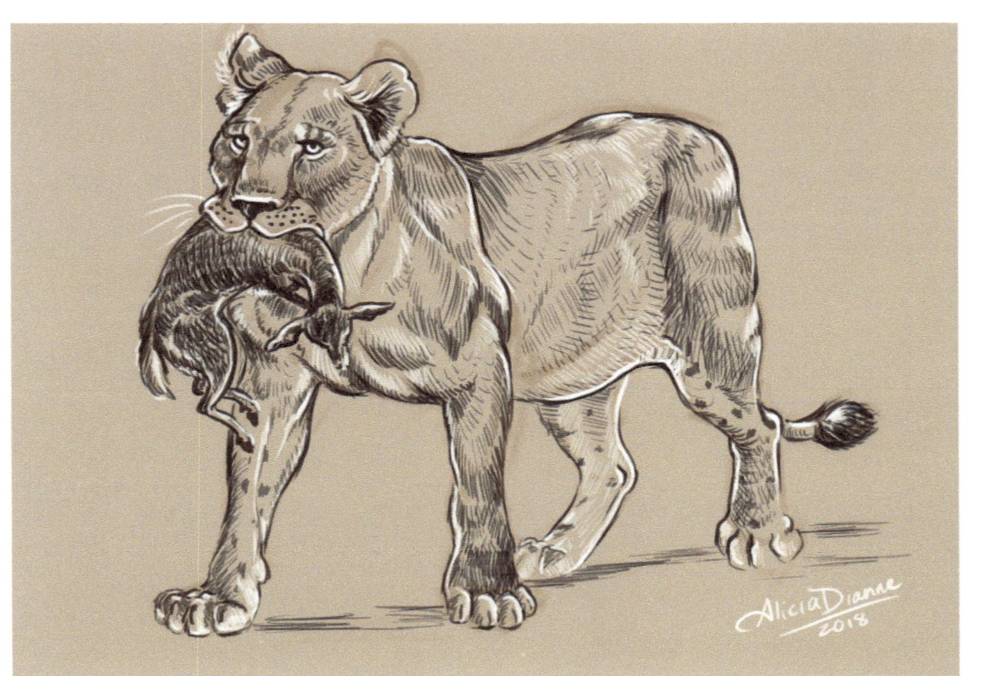

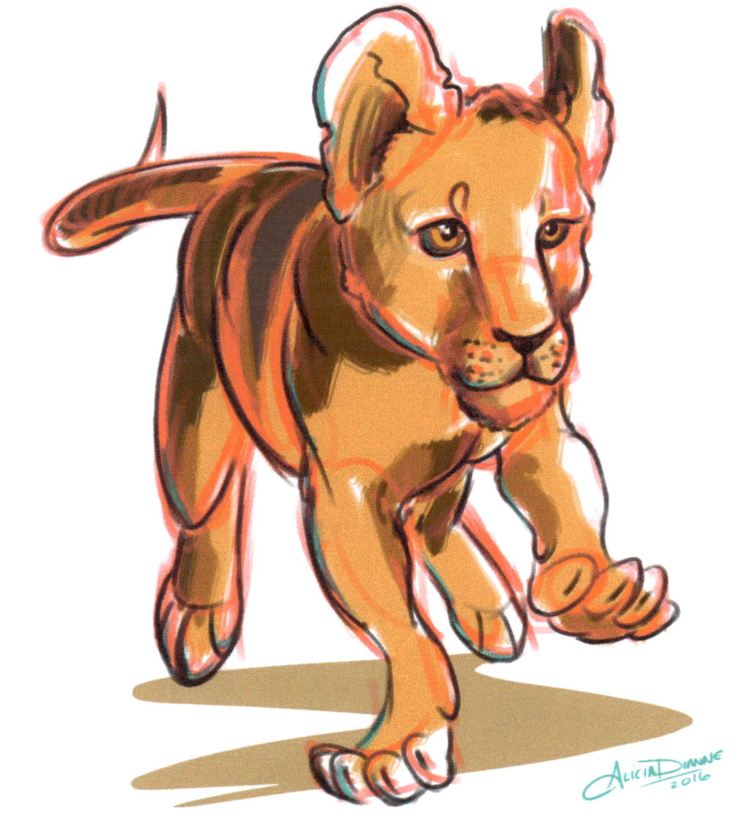

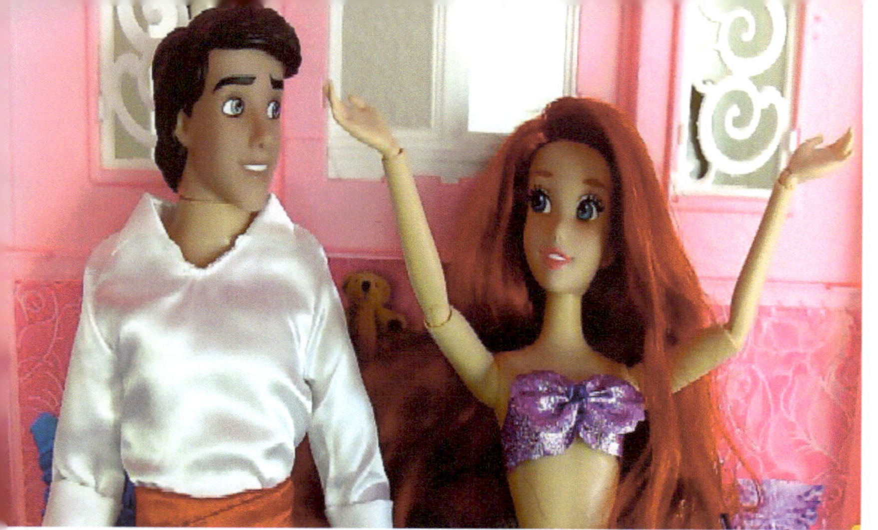

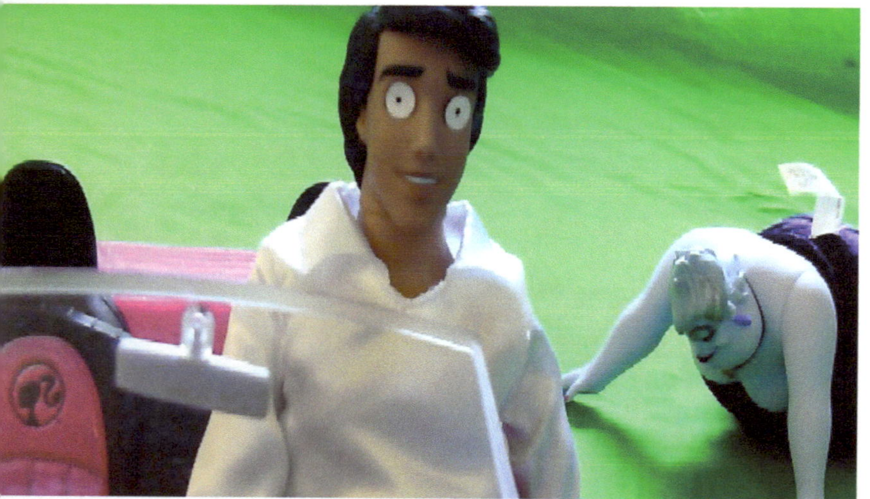

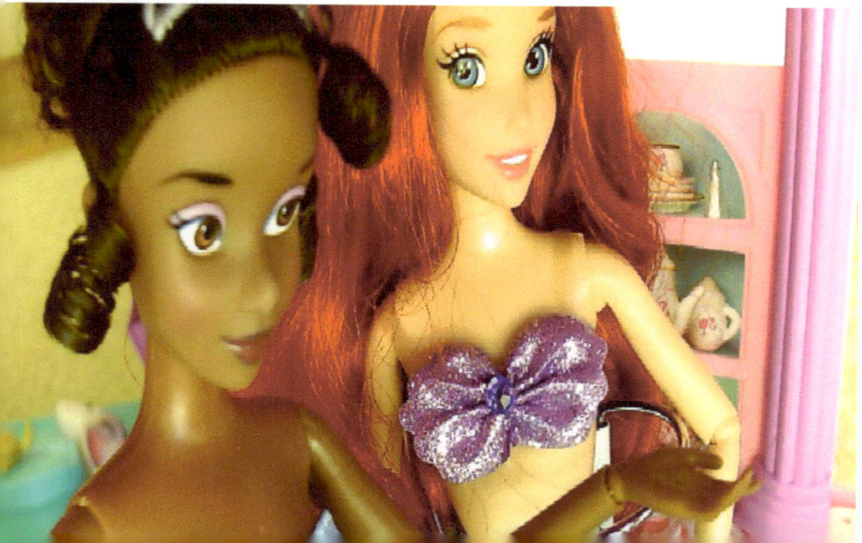

I was also introduced formal storytelling by the amazing and charming, Richard Gorey, animator and writer of *The Great Rabbit Rip-Off*. Mr. Gorey absolutely loved stories and he made writing fun! Through him, I learned subliminal ways to make a scene exciting and how to write short format scripts. However, it was now many years after SVA and I just didn't feel as comfortable telling stories, especially in longer format. I was out of practice and felt inadequate. So I developed a plan to familiarize myself with writing again. I did something that made me feel, just a *little more* comfortable. I started writing short stories.

I began with a comedic mini-series, through which I mocked my own life through the eyes of the fictional character, *"Fairiel."* I called it, *Good Girl Princess*, which was a stop-motion animated YouTube series, brought to life with my collection of *Disney* dolls. I thought it was hilarious! I can't say that it went viral or anything, but I had a ton of fun making it, and it was an exciting way to explore stories in 1-2 minute episodes.

Production Stills from *Good Girl Princess*

Next, I made *The Magic Closet*. Slightly longer, at 12 minutes, this short film allowed me to tackle an even more personal story. Using comedy and drama, this project combined the mixed media of live action film and traditional animation. Again, you may think this was procrastination. Nope! I was *maintaining momentum* and gearing up for something even bigger!

The Magic Closet was a huge growth project for me! One that I am still incredibly proud of. It took a ton of effort and allowed me to think, in terms of storytelling, in ways I simply hadn't before! Now what, might I ask, do you think was happening to my writing ability during this time? If you guessed, *getting better*, Yep! Right again! Both *The Magic Closet* and the *Good Girl Princess* series, can be seen on my YouTube channel (@AliciaDianneArt) or directly from my website, **AliciaDianne.com**

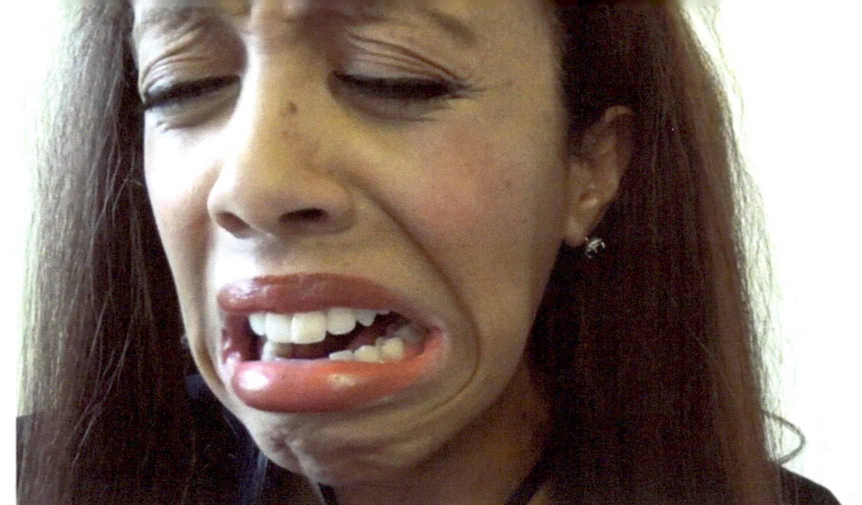

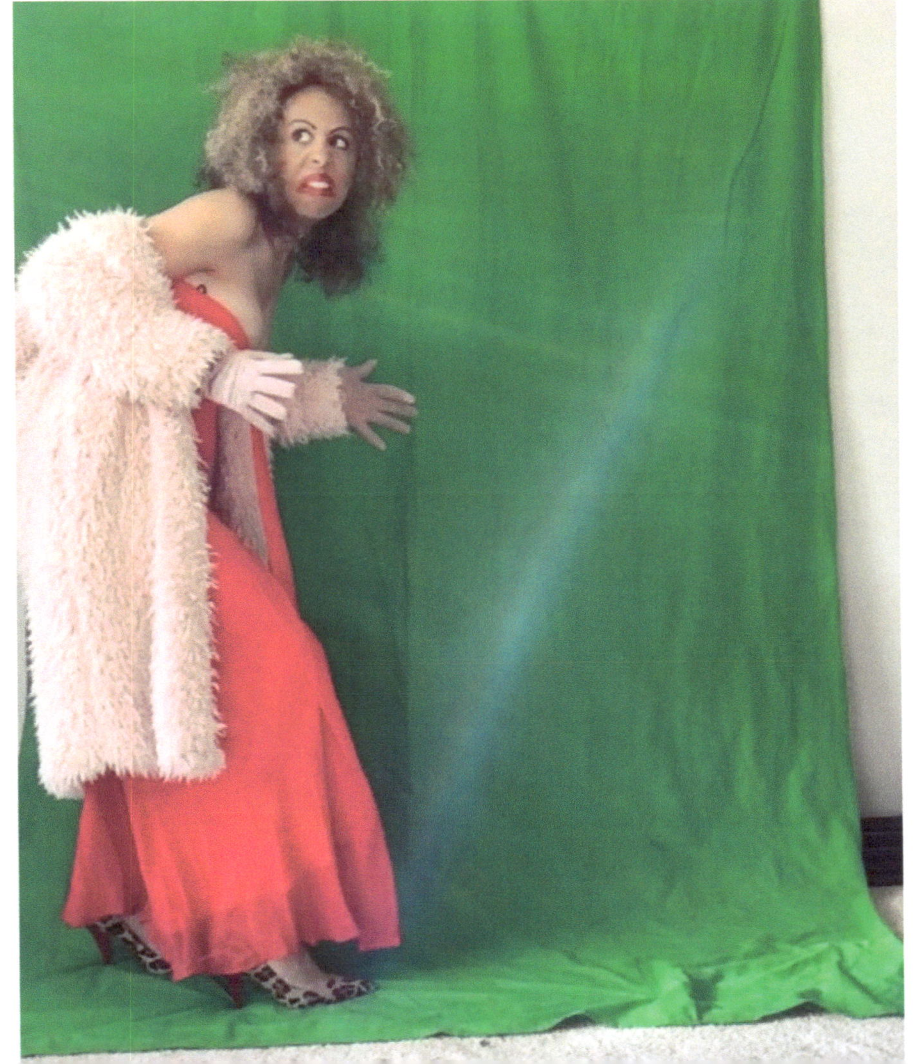

Production Stills from *The Magic Closet*

Maintain Momentum: Reflection Questions

1. On a scale of 1-10, how would you rate your confidence in your drawing ability?
2. On a scale on 1-10, how would you rate your confidence in your writing ability?
3. See the **Resource List** in the back of this book to look up "Writing Short Films."
4. Come up with 3-5 short story ideas, write them down - set a timer for 5 minutes and free write on each of them. Don't edit to start - just see what you create!
5. Sketch a few concepts of the characters for your shorts, making them as loose and scribbly or highly rendered as you like!

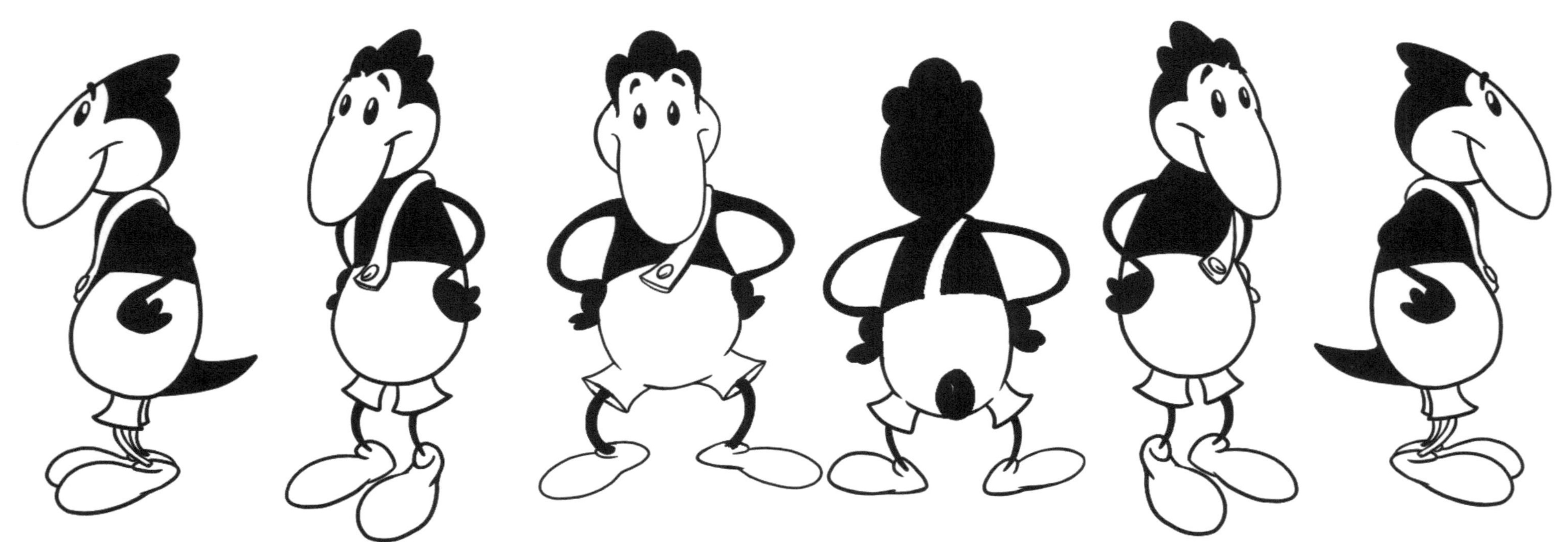

Pauly the Pangolin of *The Magic Closet*

Step 6: Three-Act Structure
is Your Friend

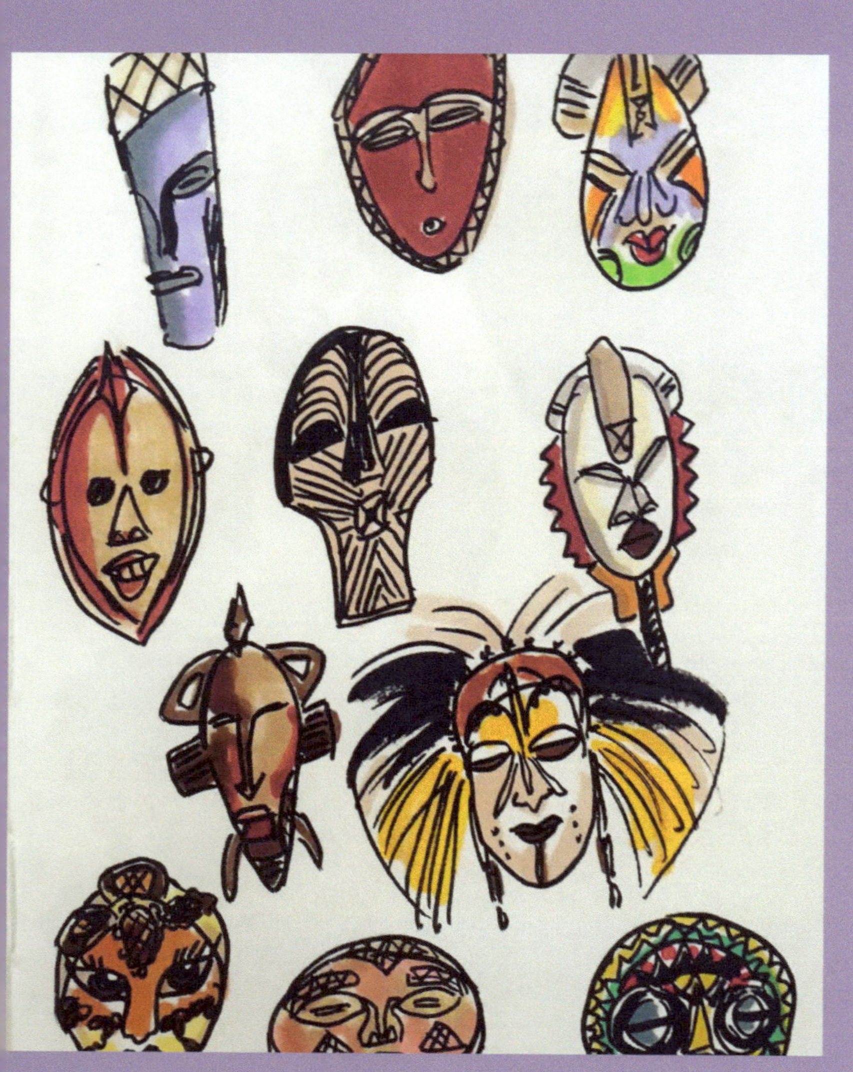

After gaining a little confidence through these smaller projects, I decided to take the plunge. There was no more dabbling to be done. I picked up my designs and character reference sheets and made the daring decision, that *I would be the one* to write *Jaydi's Story*. I would be the one to tell this story that had been floating around in my mind for years up until this point! I knew it needed to be done and that I was in fact, the right person to do it!

I began by re-familiarizing myself with 3 Act Structure. 3 Act Structure is a writing format used in storytelling and believe me, **Three-Act Structure is your friend!** Generally used in fiction, it can and is just as easily used in the telling of biographies and documentaries. It does so by dividing a story into 3 Acts: *The Setup, The Confrontation* and *The Resolution.*

- **The Setup** is your introduction. Beginning with the opening scene or, *Exposition,* it is where you, the writer, introduce your reader to the world you have built, the main characters who live in it and what ordinary life looks like for them. It is business as usual, until... the *Inciting Incident*. That thing that happens that flips everything upside down, forcing your protagonist into Act 2!

- **The Confrontation.** Your protagonist faces a series of obstacles, each with increasingly higher stakes. This section is also known as the *rising action*. It is the part of your story where your protagonist will attempt to resolve the problem brought about by the inciting incident only to realize they are not yet able to do so effectively. They must learn the skills of problem solving along the way, through their failures. This learning experience is known as your *character arc* and is usually aided with the help of a mentor or guiding force. All of the events of the rising action leads to a peak, which takes us to Act 3.

- **The Resolution.** All of that drama has led us to the *Climax* of your story! Tensions are at their highest and everything is at stake!

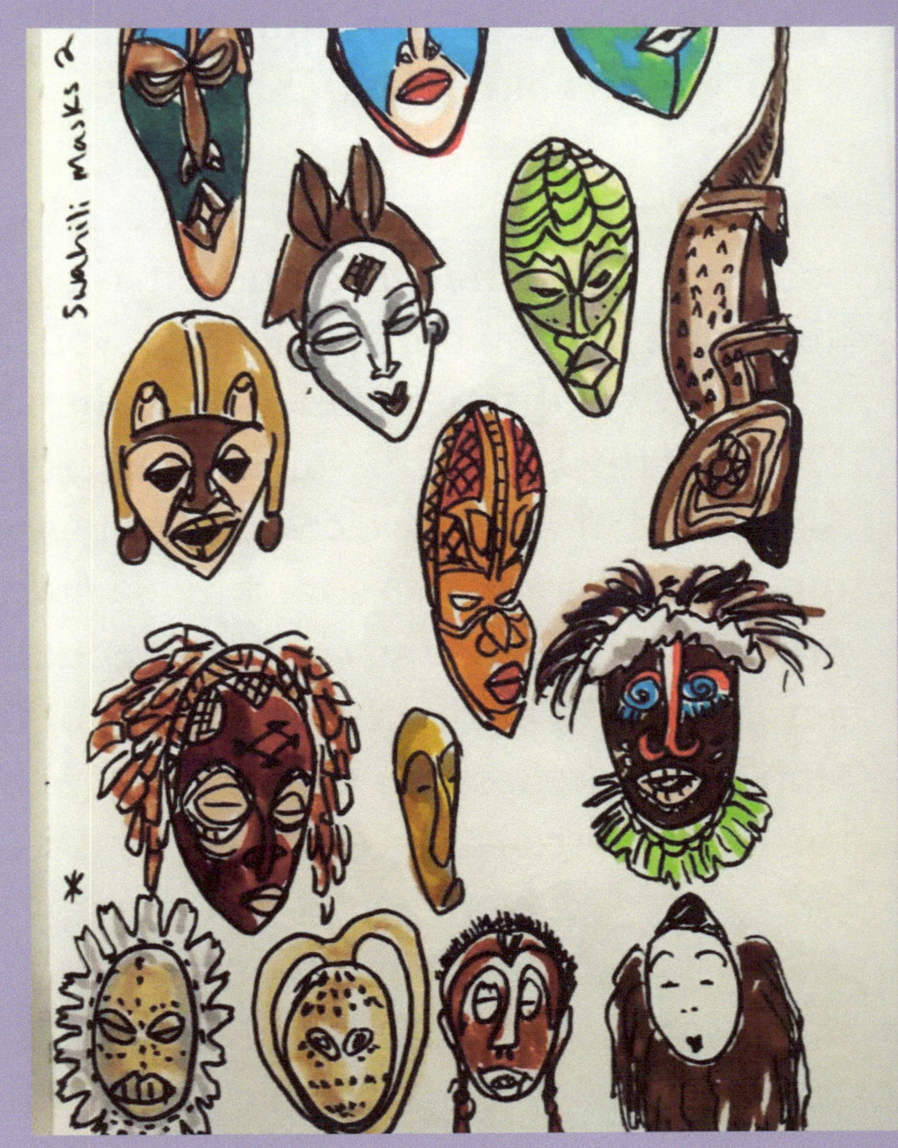

Will your protagonist succeed or fail? It's up to you! The result of either is shown in your final scene, the *Resolution*, inevitably revealing the answer to your *thematic question!*

The *Thematic Question* is the underlying *theme* of your story. It is the **moral**, posed as a question about the human experience that *you*, as the writer, get to discuss with your audience. Through the lens of the protagonist, of course! At the end of Act 3, a *successful* protagonist means they got the lesson, while a *failed* protagonist means the character couldn't take a hint and fell back on old patterns of thinking. Hopefully, the lessons your protagonist learned through the trials and obstacles of Act 2, were enough to give your guy or gal a happy ending!

But what should the thematic question be? Truthfully, you may not fully realize this until *after* the outline or even draft one is complete. So much of what we create can feel subliminal. However, knowing this, I've prepared you a bit

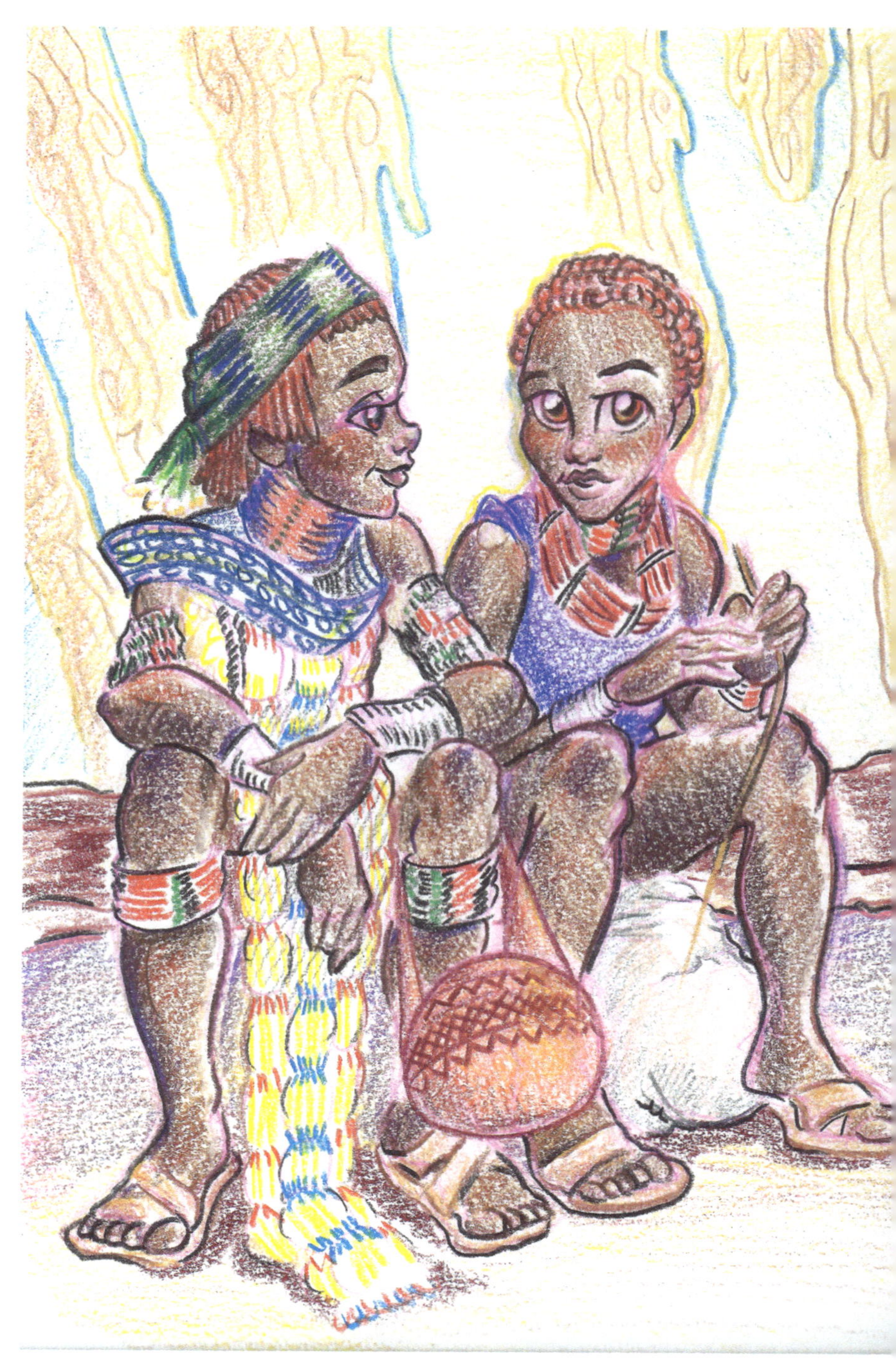

Study of Hamer Women of Ethiopia

in **Step 3**! Refer back to your Reflection Questions from that chapter, what were some of the recurring questions you received during that explorative phase? Were you able to choose a greater cause that interested you? Putting those thoughts and discoveries into question form can be a great lesson for your protagonist (and audience) to learn through your story! For *Jaydi's Story*, I came up with the thematic question: *"Is it possible to follow Western Religion while also being Spiritually Liberated?"*

What does that mean? Well, I wanted to make sense of my faith with the new knowledge I had been discovering while researching African History. Not the *cliff-notes* version, but a more complete realization that indeed Christianity had been used out of context to justify many evils. It had been used incorrectly to colonize nations, to infiltrate communities and scout resources, as well as to force people to conform into Western ways of life and in some instances, yes, to justify slavery. [*Editors, Charles River, The Scramble for Africa. CreateSpace Independent Publishing Platform, 2017*]

The reason I knew it had been used out of context is because I had actually read *The Holy Bible* for myself, from *Genesis* to *Revelations*, so I knew the actual truth of which I placed my faith. However, this conflict was something I wanted to address. It was now becoming more evident to me, through my research of African History, that I wanted to address these issues within the context of *Jaydi's Story*. Does your thematic question need to be equally pressing? Short answer, no. Just so long as it is feels *meaningful* to you. That is the point here, find within yourself ***an authentic experience of life*** that you wish to express as your *big idea*, which will motivate you through to the end! This is why the **Research** portion of **Step 4** is so important. So make sure that you don't skip this crucial part of your process! When you feel confident about your world and your characters, you'll be ready to create an *Outline*. Your outline is where you can identify, in a sentence or two, all of your key plot points, which will later become scenes. Begin with these 4: ***Exposition, Inciting Incident, Climax***, and ***Resolution*** - then you can expand on those ideas. There are many ways to do this, but the way I found worked for me in this process, was by using *The Hero's Journey* format. The Hero's Journey is a writing format that is divided into 12 stages:

1. *Ordinary World - (Exposition)*
2. *Call to Adventure - (Inciting Incident)*
3. *Refusal of the Call*
4. *Meeting the Mentor*
5. *Crossing the Threshold*
6. *Tests, Allies, Enemies*
7. *Approach the Inmost Cave*
8. *The Ordeal*
9. *Reward / Seizing the Sword*
10. *The Road Back*
11. *Resurrection - (Climax)*
12. *Return with Elixir - (Resolution)*

There are variations, but in the format I chose, *Stages 1-4* compose Act 1. *Stages 5-9* compose Act 2 and *Stages 10-12* compose Act 3. It should be noted that Acts 1 and 3 each

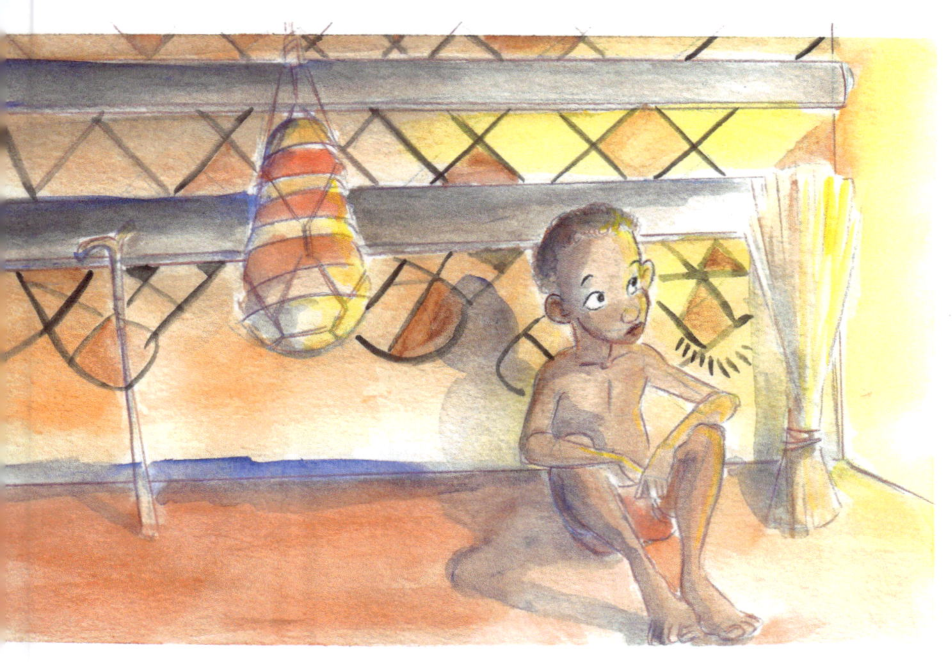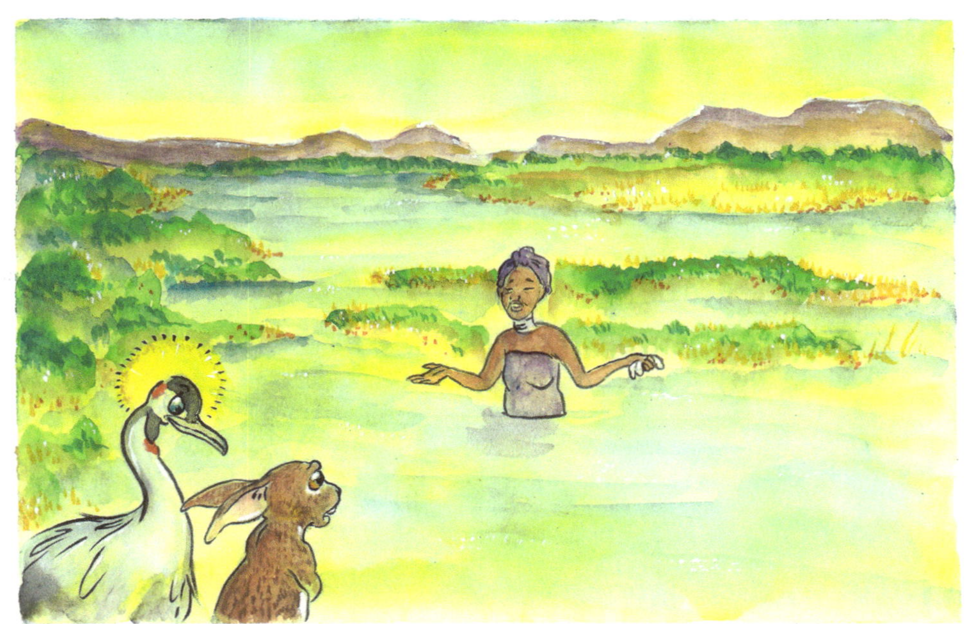

take up about 25% of your story, while Act 2 takes the remaining 50%. This 1-12 format allows you to easily divide your story into 12 parts, which you can compose of in scenes. This format is believed to have first been used as long ago as 7th-8th century B.C. in the Ancient Greek tale of *The Odyssey* written by Homer. It was brought into the mainstream by Joseph Campbell's *The Hero with a Thousand Faces,* written in 1949, and has been used perhaps thousands of times to create a *pattern of storytelling* with which audiences are familiar. However, this does not limit the storyteller by any means! Your story will be completely your own! *You decide* what you want to happen, how it will happen, and to whom it will happen! Your outline will work as a guiding light for you as you work your way to making your very first draft.

Once your outline is complete, review it. Notice the *theme* that may already be looking back at you. Explore ideas and revise your outline. The next stage is to just start writing.

Set a time, every day, and commit to writing whatever your goal is for that day. For me, it was a set a period of time, which I set for an hour each day just to write. Some days I wrote more, some days not as much. Most imporantly, I was able to get to a point where I committed to doing it everyday. As a warning here, do not let a missed day be treated as a debt. Do not double the time of your next day's work or engage in any negative self talk, this will only delay the process! Treat writing as a new habit, do it at the same time, in the same place, each time. Pick an amount of time or work you can commit to. Celebrate your progress by rewarding yourself with a simple *(healthy)* pleasure each time you meet your goal. Eventually, you will get to that last scene - that closing line of dialogue - and that in itself, is one of the greatest rewards of all.

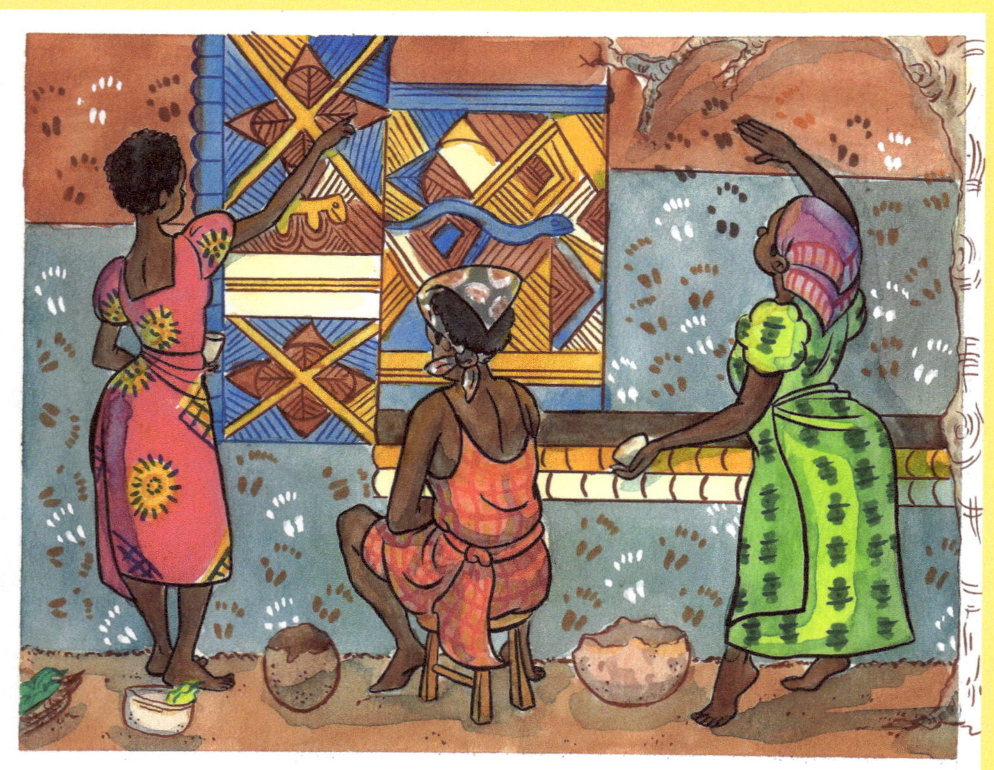

Studies (from left) Nigerian Women, Maasai Boys and Himba Boy with cows

3 Act Structure is Your Friend: Reflection Questions

1. Create a simple sketch for the **Exposition, Inciting Incident, Climax** and **Resolution** of your story. Write a few sentences about your ideas for each.
2. Expand on those ideas by outlining your story into the 12 steps of the Hero's Journey or other format of your choice. Create a simple sketch and write your ideas for each.
3. Brainstorm some possible *Thematic Questions* - the moral at the core of your story that will teach a lesson. What is the *conversation* you want to have with your audience about your chosen subject matter?
4. What weakness or flaw can you give your protagonist to overcome through the ordeals of Act 2 in order to be successful (or not) in Act 3? Explain it in a sentence or two.
5. Review your outline and revise it based on your new insights.
6. No going back now! Write your first draft! You can do it!

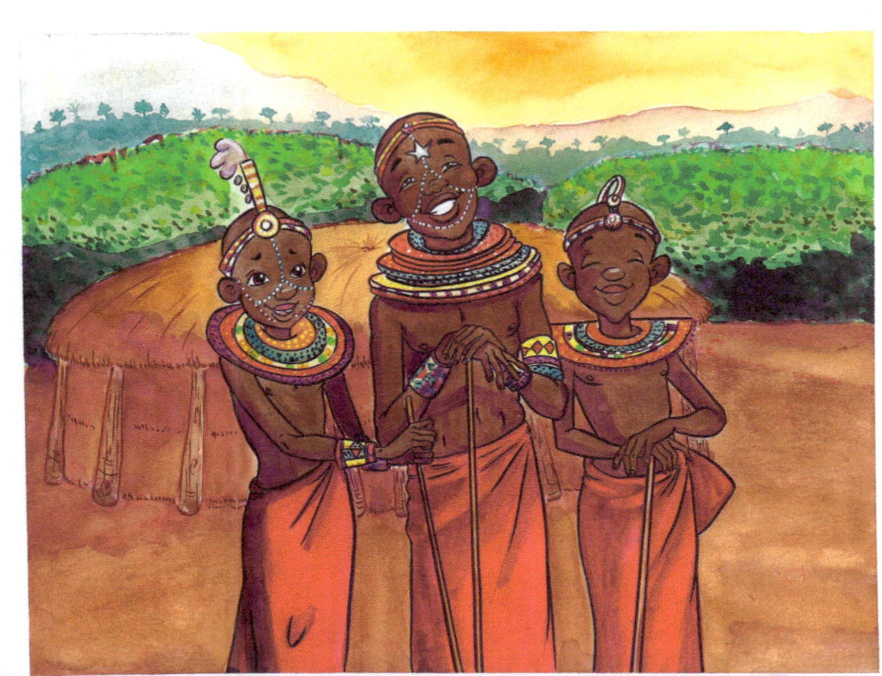

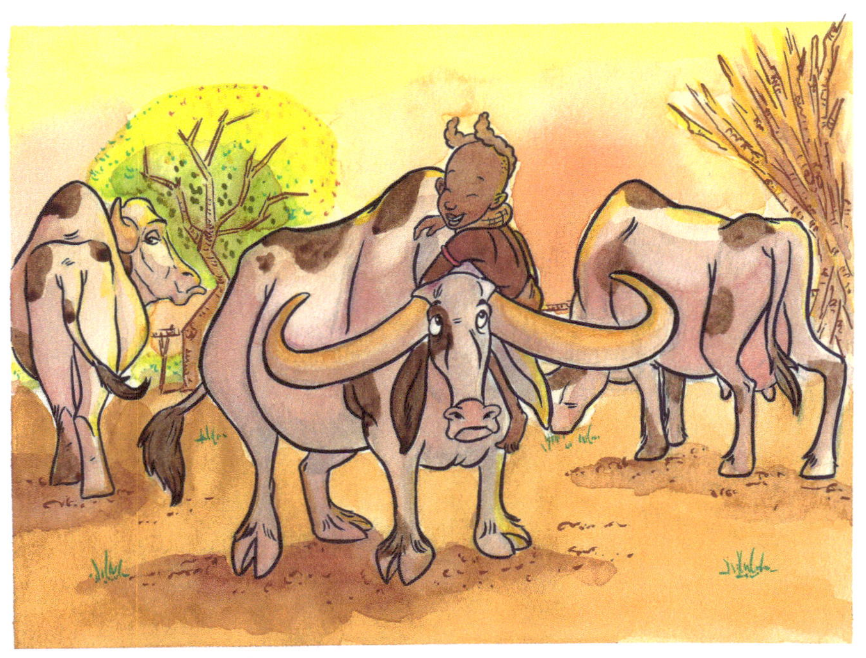

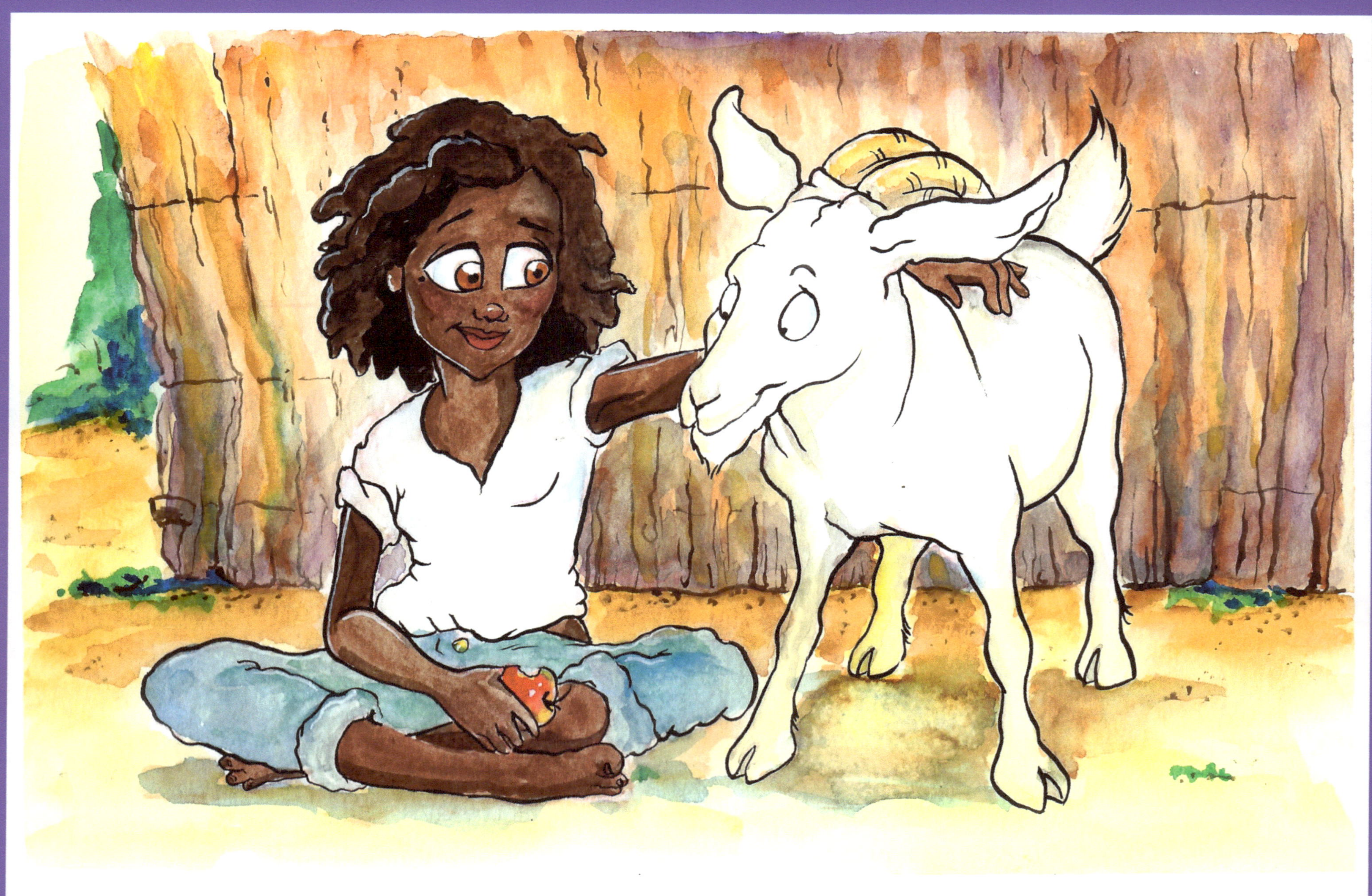

Early concept of *Jaydi* and *Atsukpi*

Step 7: The Creative Process

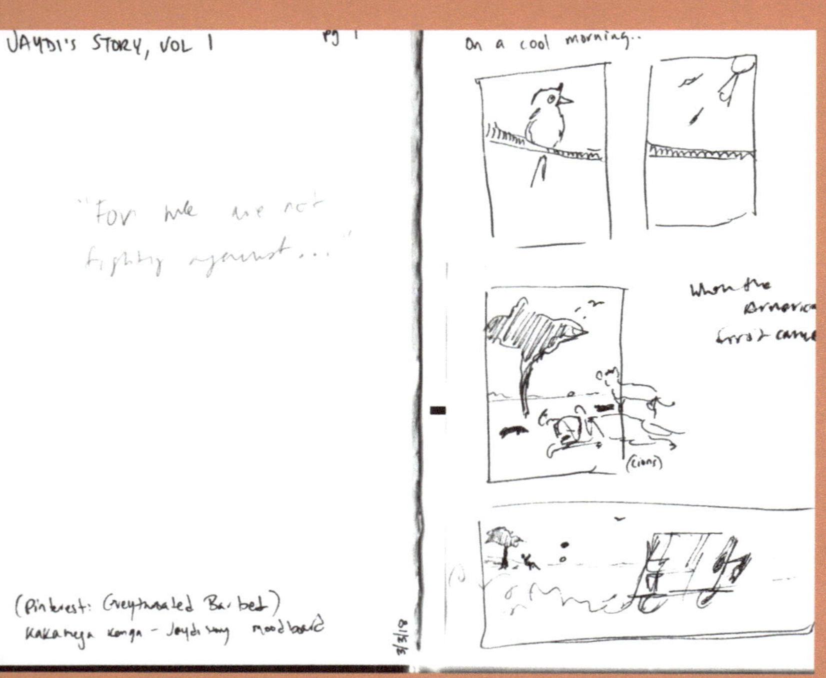

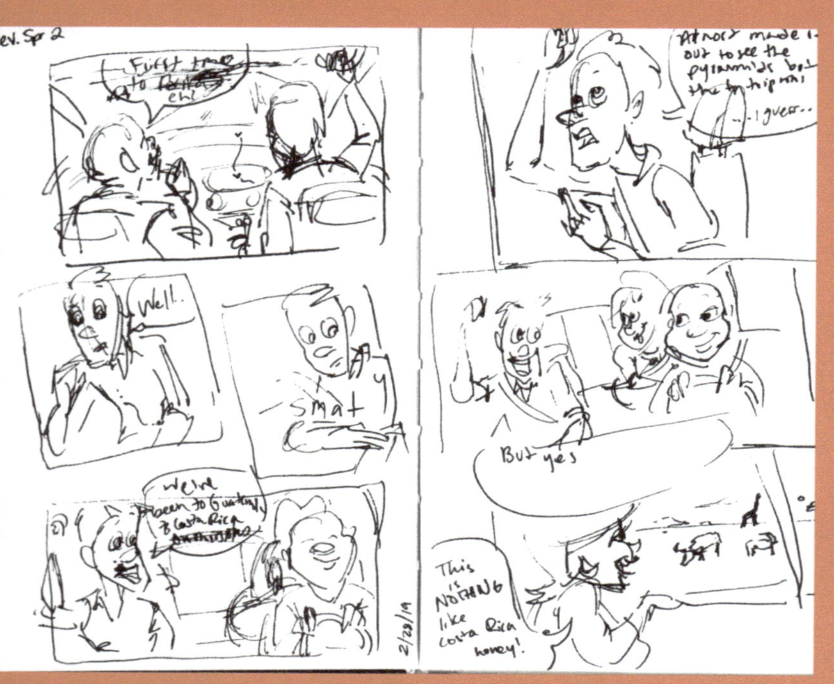

Since I have brought up so many artists who've influenced me, I would be beyond amiss if I did not mention Jason Brubaker. Brubaker is a talented graphic novelist who also has an incredibly helpful YouTube channel. I learned about Jason from another of my favorite YouTubers - character designer, Will Terrell. Jason was a guest on Will's channel showing a demo of how he colored a short comic strip Will had drawn. I loved his style and personality, and decided to check out some of the videos from his own channel, *Coffee Table Comics*. I was blown away by Jason's not only creative skill, but sentiment of storytelling. What I loved even more, was his willingness to discuss his *faith*, and how it had inspired his comics, particularly in his series, *Sithrah*.

I bought the first volume of *Sithrah* and became hooked! I blew through the entire series, which is currently still available on *WebToons*, where Brubaker was a featured contributor. His influence is literally what made me decide to turn *Jaydi's Story* from the concept of an illustrated book into a

Graphic Novel series. And yes, this decision was made *after* the first draft! It didn't matter, his guidance played a big part in helping me take the first steps of **the creative phase** for my first graphic novel. Eventually, I would find many more amazing comic artists to be inspired by.

You may or may not need a slew of outlets to pull from for your first book. It is my hope that through this writing, you have a much fuller picture than I had to start out with. That this book streamlines the process a bit, removing some of the mystery. If you still have unanswered questions, continue to seek them out! The goal is that *you* successfully create your own graphic novel and through that, tell a story that is meaningful to you!

Up until now, I'd been talking mostly about story. Because, let us be honest here, without a story there are no panels to be drawn, rendered or colored. Plus, without a meaningful theme, what's the point? The *creative* phase is the final

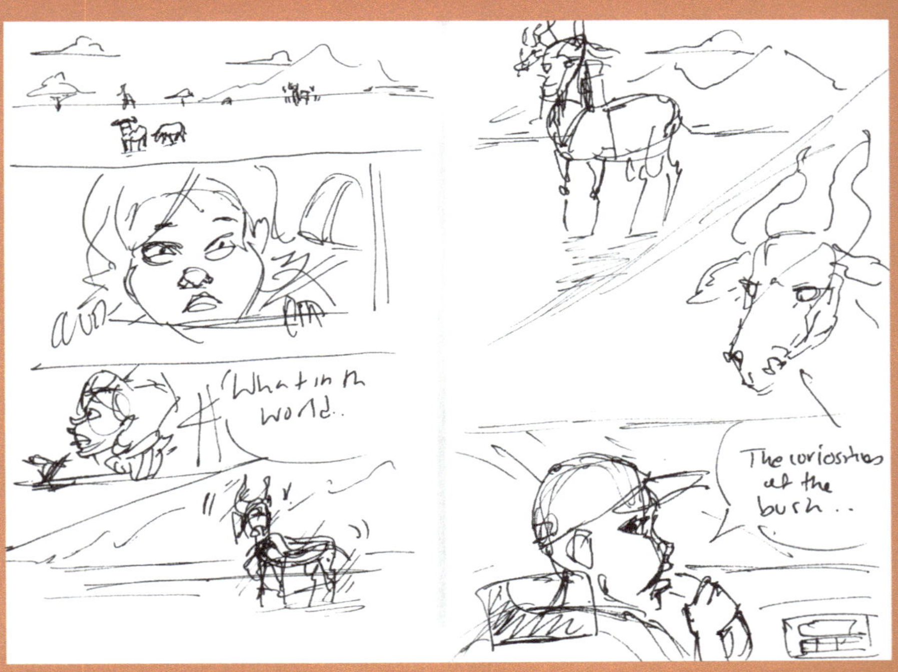

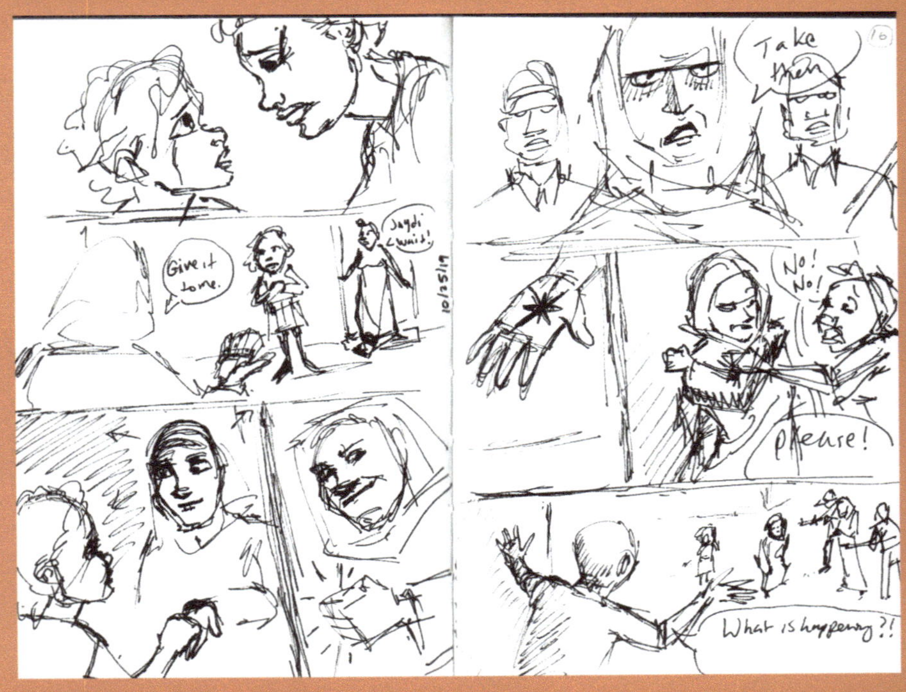

stage that brings it all to life! The best way that I've found to approach this phase, is by dividing into 6 parts:

1. *Thumbnails*
2. *Penciling*
3. *Clean line / Inking*
4. *Flatting*
5. *Light & Shadow*
6. *Lettering*

Let's explore each one of these parts in a little more detail, shall we? **Thumbnails** are typically small, loose drawings. They get the name from just that, artists prepared "thumbnail-sized" drawings to plan for a more sophisticated painting or drawing. Did anyone ever draw their thumbnails the size of an *actual thumbnail?* Probably not, in my experience, most artists draw them at about 3"x4" or so. These can be done traditionally or digitally, this is your call! The main idea is to plan the composition of the shot, which will eventually represent a panel,

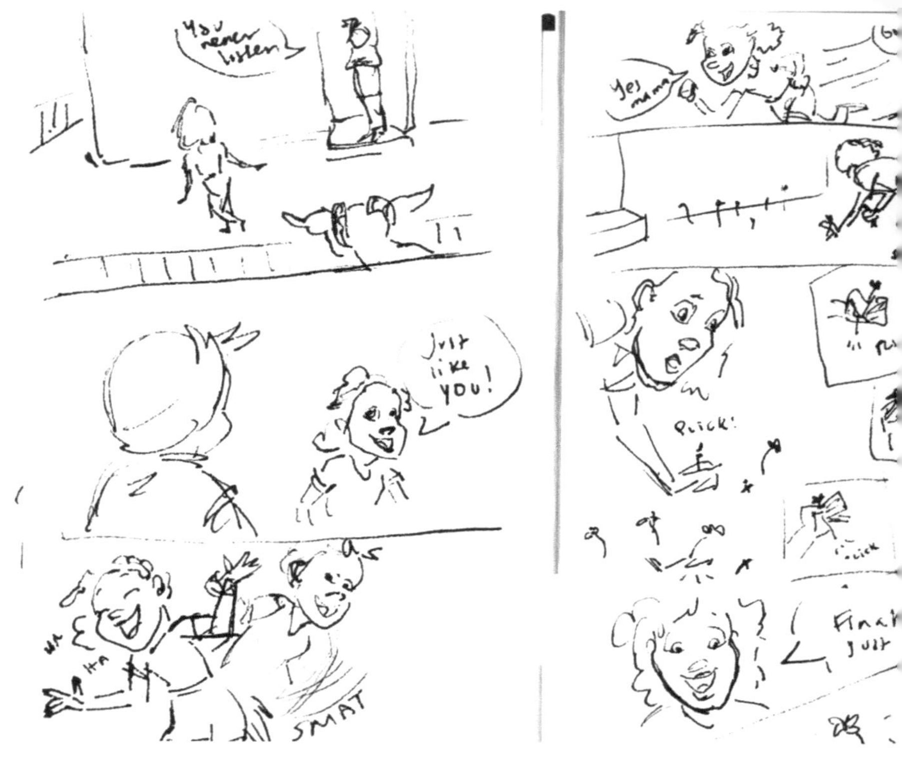

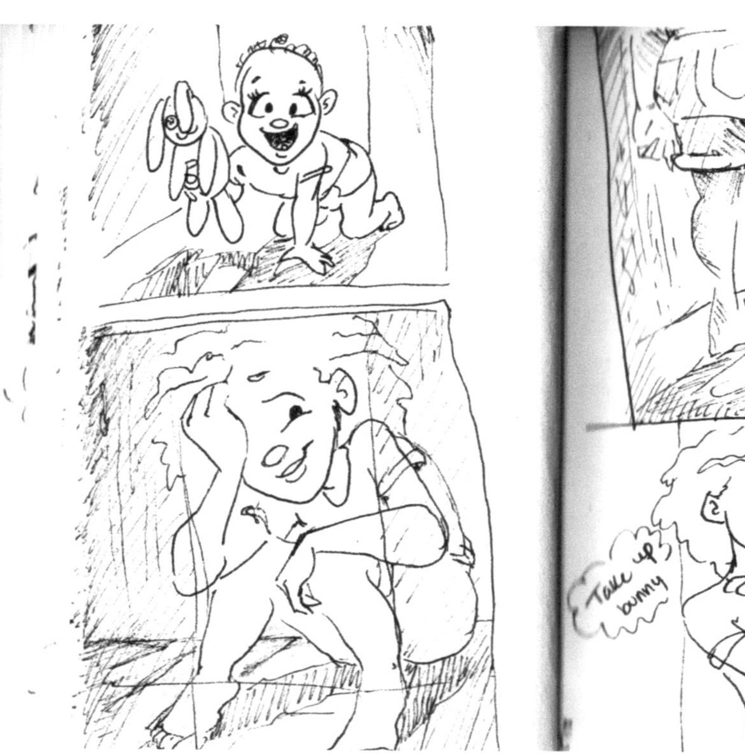

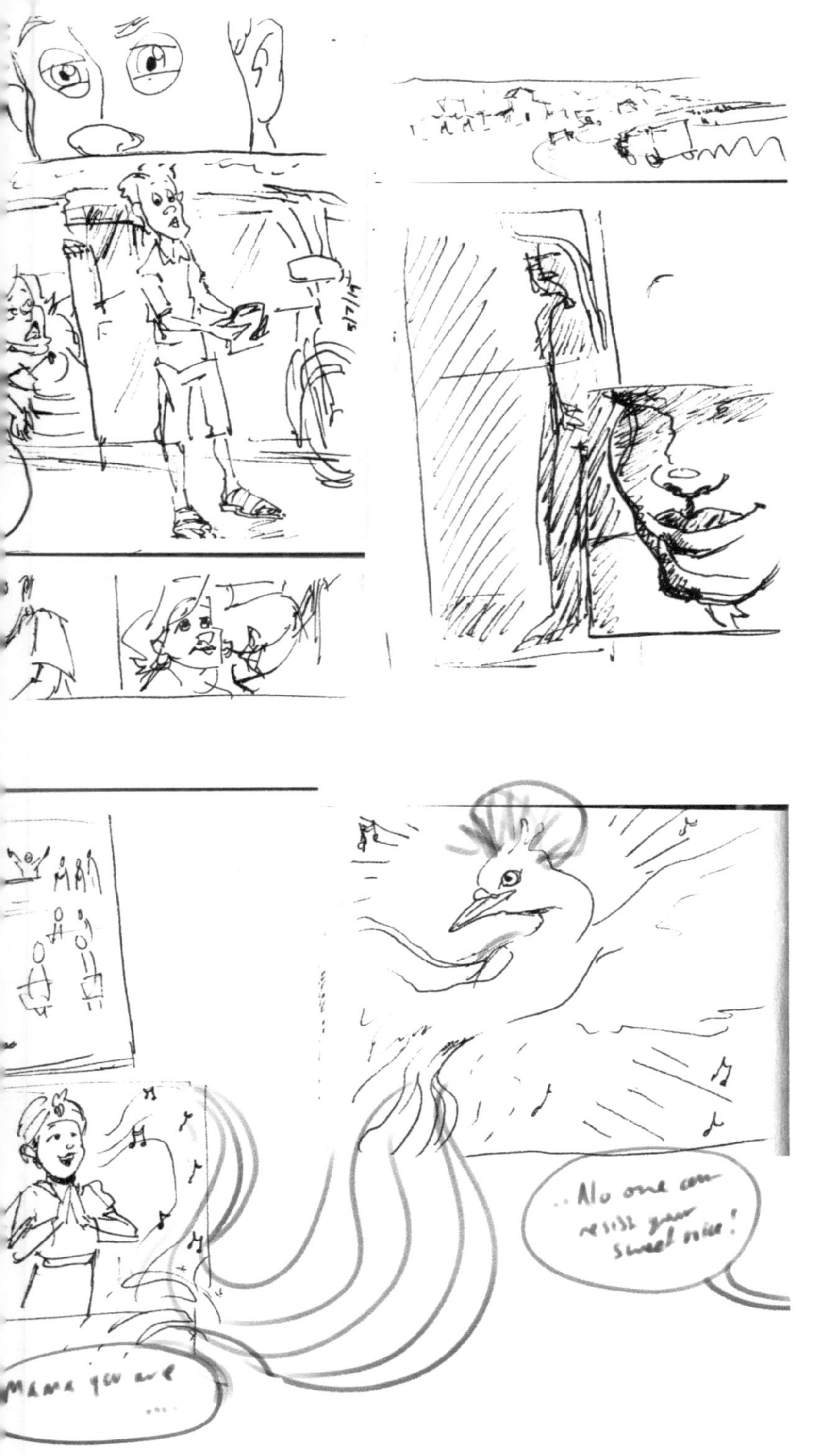

or individual frame. One thing you want to make sure of, is that you include room for your text and dialogue. This can be easy to forget, but it's very important that you are aware of what's being said, so you can provide adequate space. You do want your reader to know what's being said, don't you? After all, as they say, *clarity is key*. That being said, you want to make sure that your story is as clear as possible *without* any dialogue. That may sound counter-intuitive to the tip I just gave, but it's actually not! Your job is to make understanding the story as *clear* as possible. Always keep in mind that, like a movie, a graphic novel is a *visual medium*, make your shots clear!

During the **Penciling** stage, you will clean up your shots by refining your drawings and making them more clear. You will also want to organize your panels to fit a *template*. A template? Yes! You will need to have your imagery align in a way that makes sense from page to page. If you are using standard comic size, this will be 6.625"x10.25" with an additional 0.25" on either side for *print bleed*,

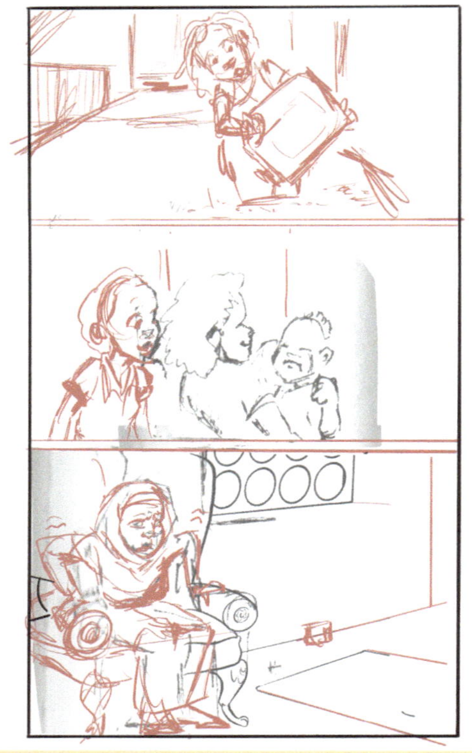

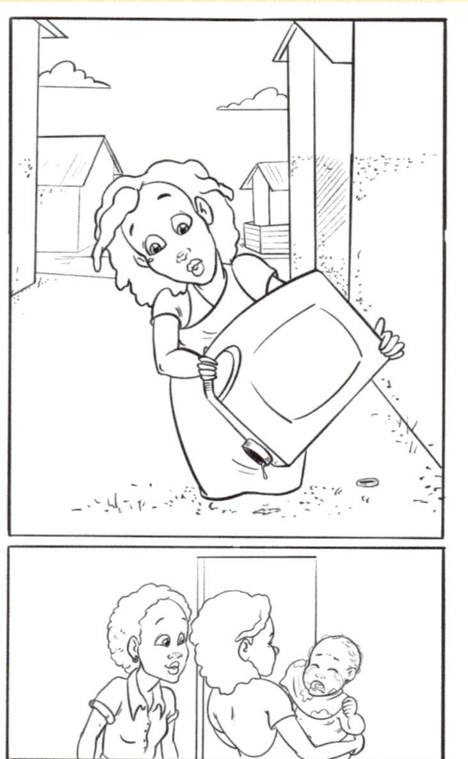

extra space if you decide to have your book physically printed. Create a space within that barrier to use as a *page* or *spread template* so that your layout will make sense sense from page to page. As long as you have a template, you can play around as much as you want with panel shapes and sizes, just keep them within the barrier! The only exception is when you create a *splash page* - a single panel that takes up an entire page or a *two-page spread*, at which point your illustration can extend beyond the barriers and into the bleed. Depending on the way you work, your **Clean line** and your **Inking** may be one in the same. For me they were two different steps, but a very similar process. I had created my thumbnails traditionally and penciled digitally. I also applied a clean line digitally, in order to have a crisp space for which to add color. Whatever you decide, apply your clean and/or inked line with care, as this is your finalized line.

Flatting is the application of flat color, also know as *local color*. Local color is the natural color of each object, untouched by light. Flatting is the first part of the coloring phase, so you can then decide where and how to place the light and shadow depending on the light source.

In the **Light & Shadow** phase, you will determine your *source of light* for each panel (whether on screen or off). Your source of light can be any variety of things, from the sun, to a lamp, headlights on a car, or the moon. These light sources will determine where light is coming from and the inevitable shadows cast by each object in the frame.

For **Lettering**, you'll want to streamline the process as much as possible. Just remember, lettering is *LAST!* You won't make any speech bubbles until AFTER your illustrations are complete! I had to learn this the hard way! There are a number of programs you can use, but for this process specifically, I prefer Adobe Photoshop. Use the *marquee tool* to create the shape for your speech bubble and add a *fin* (the point connecting the bubble to the character speaking) with the *lasso tool*. As long as you have both bubble and fin on the same layer, you can double click that layer and add the *effect* or *Layer Style,* "Stroke," which will outline your bubble. Play around with thickness and color, I use about a 2-4 pixel stroke in black. Also, I've found it easier to type the text in each panel *first, (USING ALL CAPS for ease of reading),*

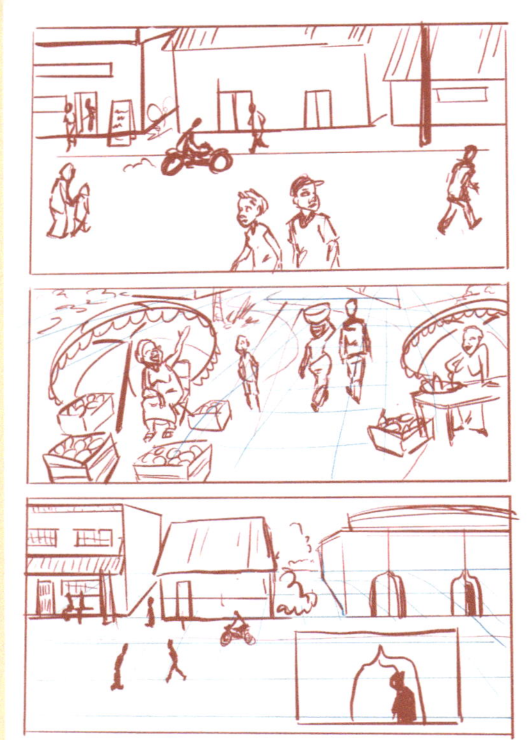

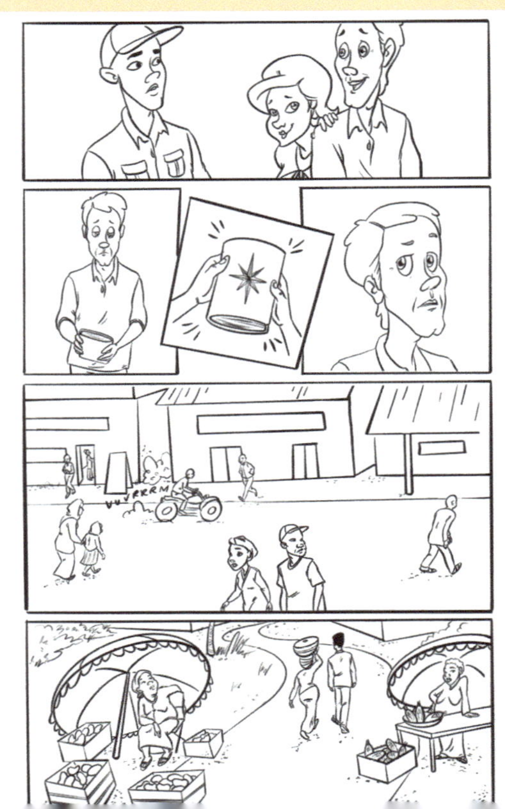

and then transforming my bubble to fit the text. Remember, *clarity is key!*

The Creative Phase: Reflection Questions

1. Select one page from your first draft to thumbnail.
2. Create a standard comic-sized document (6.625"x10.25") in the drawing app or platform of your choice, using 300 dpi. Remember to include room for page bleed (0.25").
3. Including a template space for your panels, layout the thumbnails.
4. On a new layer, cleanup your drawings, adding ink and color if you like.
5. Experiment with speech bubbles and include at least one speech bubble on your new page.

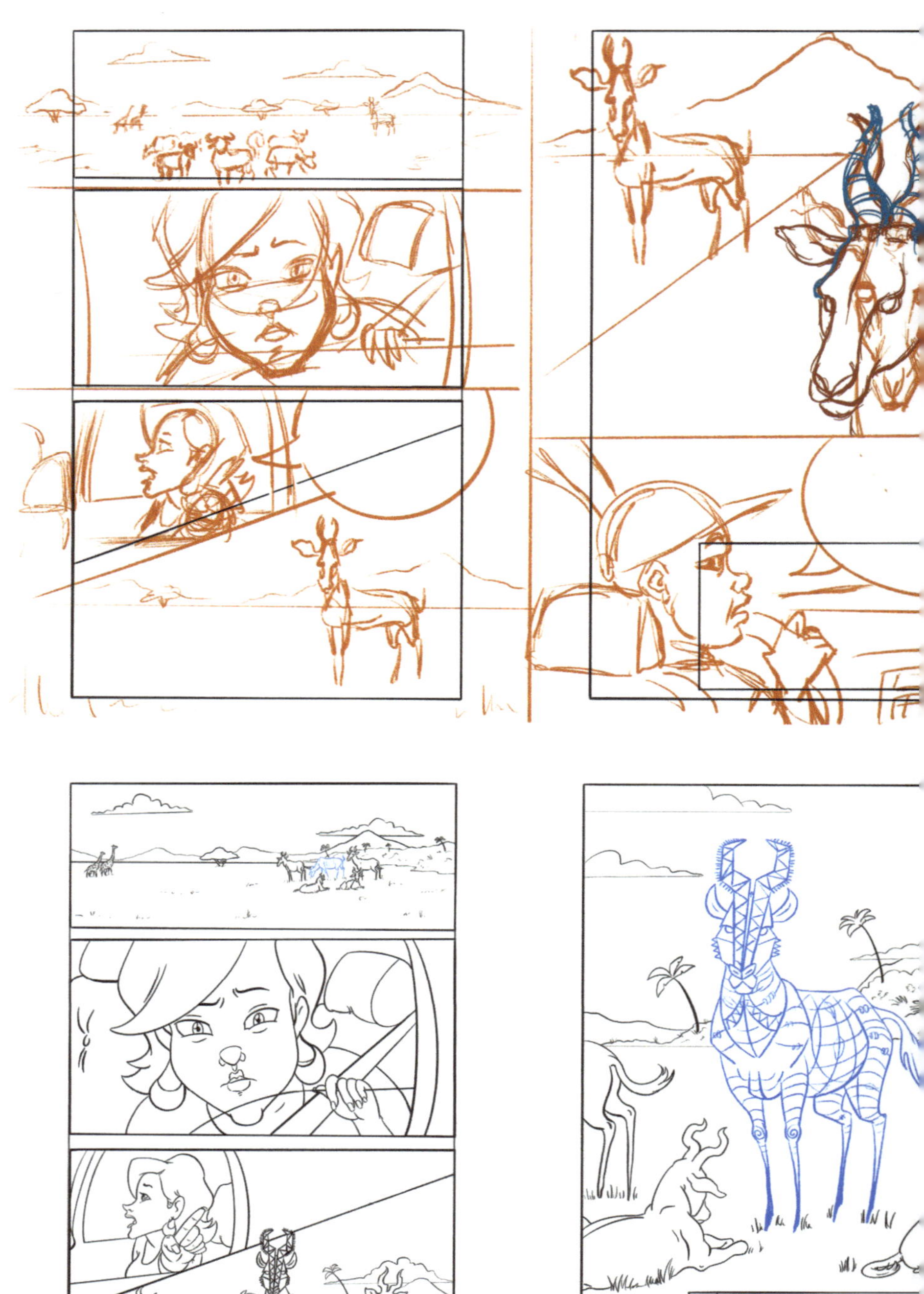

Step 8: Get Feedback

Feedback. This, undoubtedly, can be the most challenging part of the process. *But* it can provide you with major insight into what you need to work on. During the time I'd begun working on the first draft of *Jaydi's Story*, I had entered into graduate school. Deciding to study MA Illustration at California State University at Northridge (CSUN).

I knew I would work on my big graphic novel project while I was there, however I didn't know what that would look like. I imagined I would allow my ideas to unfold with the nurturing guidance of my helpful professors. Not exactly.

My committee of professors, as it would turn out, were of the formal, *Fine Art* world. This initially did not intimidate me at all, as I had always considered myself a fine artist. I didn't realize though, that to them, as well as a number of others in the *Avant-Garde* community, Illustration, let alone comics, was considered rather *low in rank* on the formal art

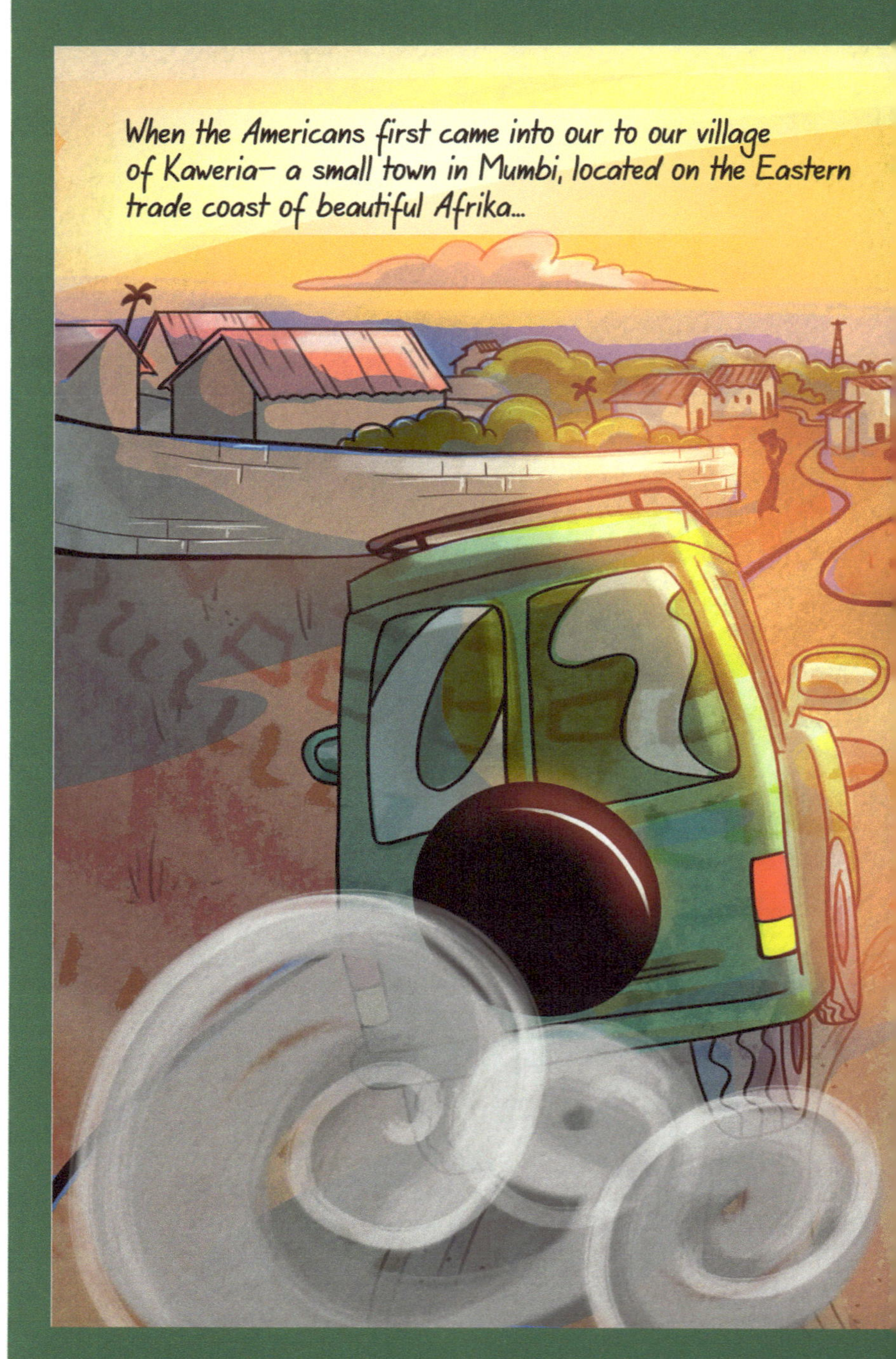

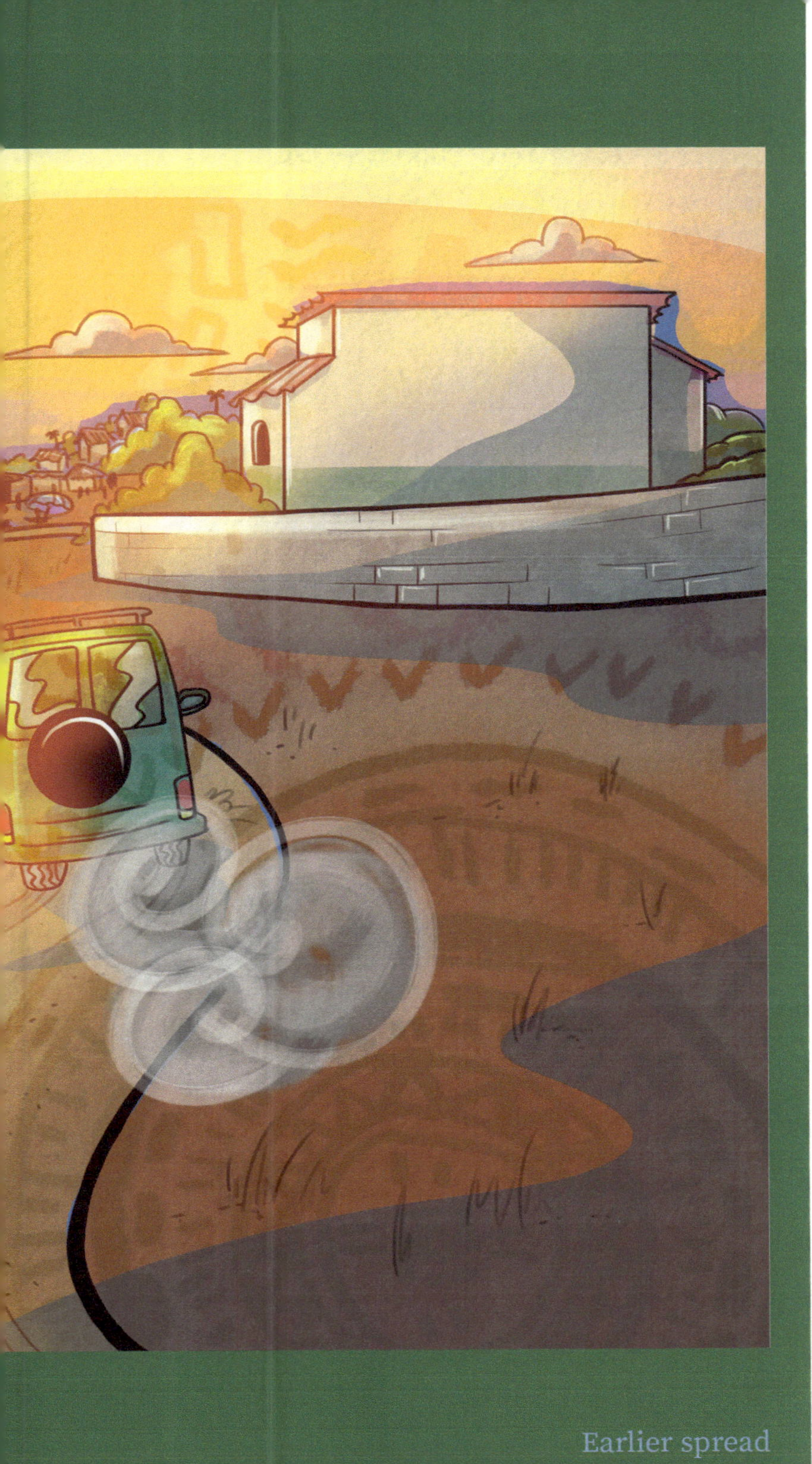

scale. To many, illustration is less of a *fine art* but rather a *commercial art*. I disagreed.

So be it, I make cartoons and I am proud of it. But I'd decided that in no way, shape or form was I going to allow my work to be viewed as a *lesser* art. I challenged my professors, a lot, some times. I refused *bend the knee* and let them force the label on me that they were intending to place. A label known as *"Kitsh." Kitsh* is German term, one that literally means *"trash."* The term became popular for *"cheap art"* in the early 20th century. So in my first committee critique, what do you think happened? I was eaten alive…

I wasn't prepared to speak on my art and stand up for it - so they ripped me to shreds. They questioned my motive… the writing, the use of religion. They called it *"Propaganda!"* They even asked me why I bothered coming to Grad School if I was going to make comics. *Ouch!* For all of the remarks I heard that day, I was not prepared for any of them. Shortly after it was all over... I broke down. Not a moment after they left the room, I fell into tears and had to call my husband to mop me up off of the floor. I simply, wasn't ready. I'd like to say that I promptly picked myself up and went back to the drawing board, but it was not so. For months thereafter, I didn't draw at all.

"Well damn." You might say, *"Why should I ask anyone what they think of my work if that is the result?"* Because, my friend, although I was in fact defeated temporarily, this harsh feedback was the best possible thing that could have happened for me and *Jaydi's Story* up to that point. I had experienced *complete* humiliation, yet somehow, it allowed me to realize

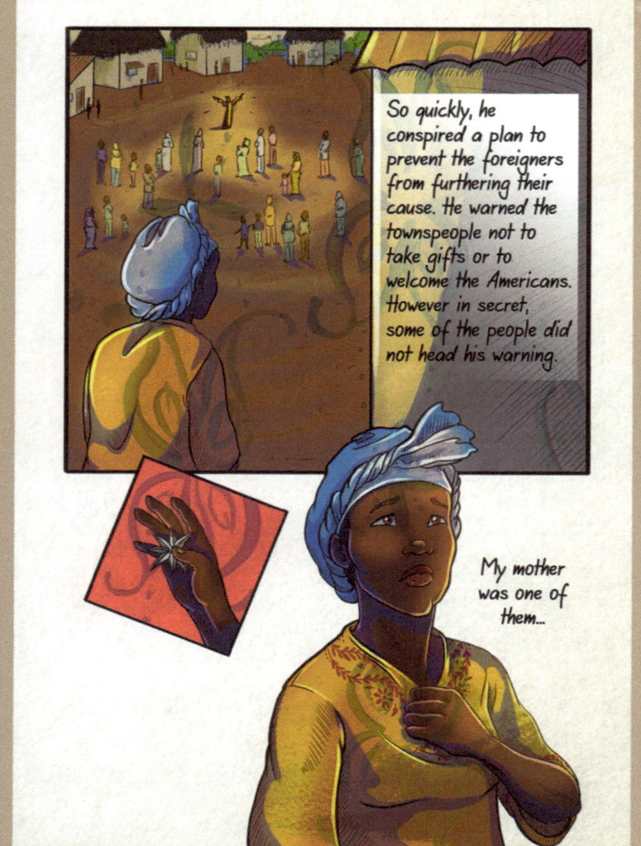

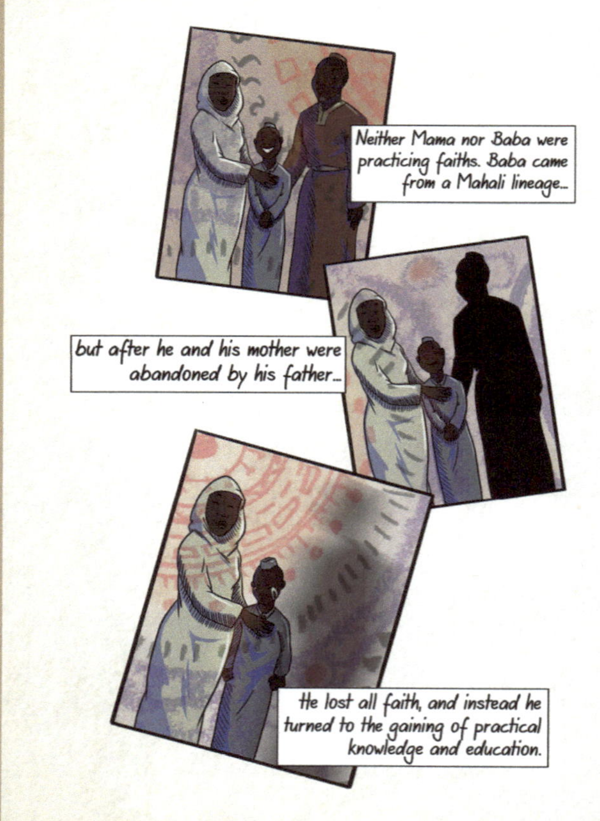

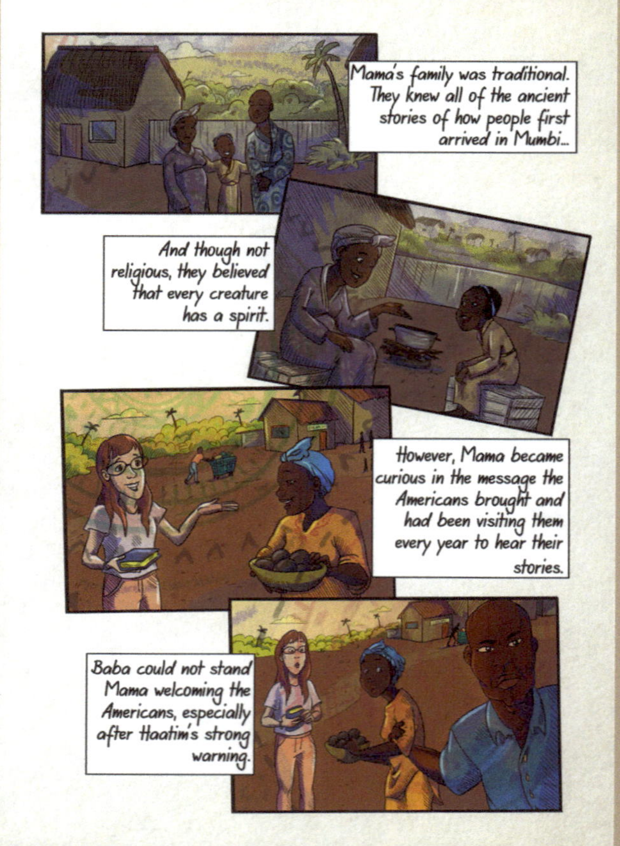

how much I really did care about this project, and still do! It allowed me to think, *"Yes, I've worked hard, but how can I work harder?" "What don't I know that I need to know, in order to defend my work?" "How can I 'Twirl on My Haters'?"* as the fabulous Beyoncé might say? So please, **Get Feedback!** It may hurt in the moment, but if you use the experience in the right way, you'll be ready for the next step!

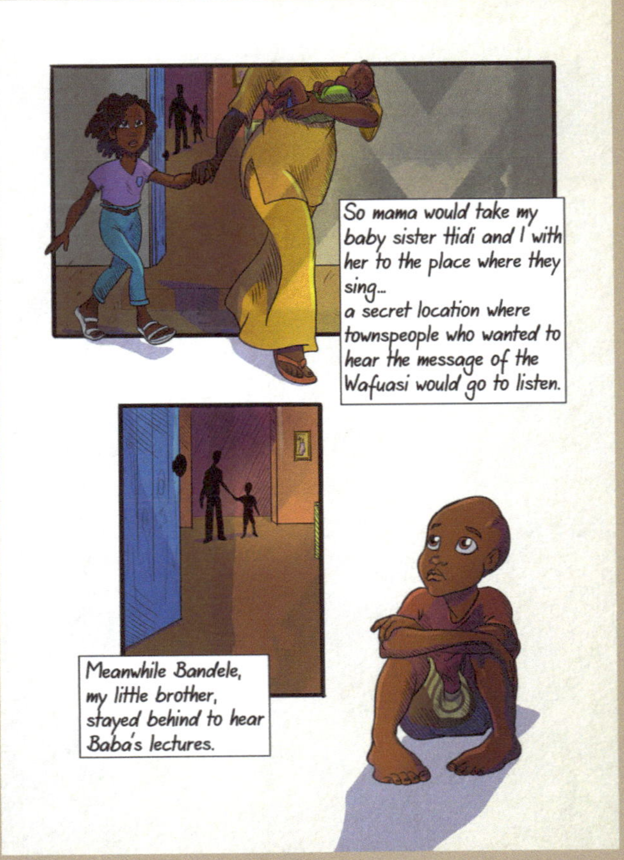

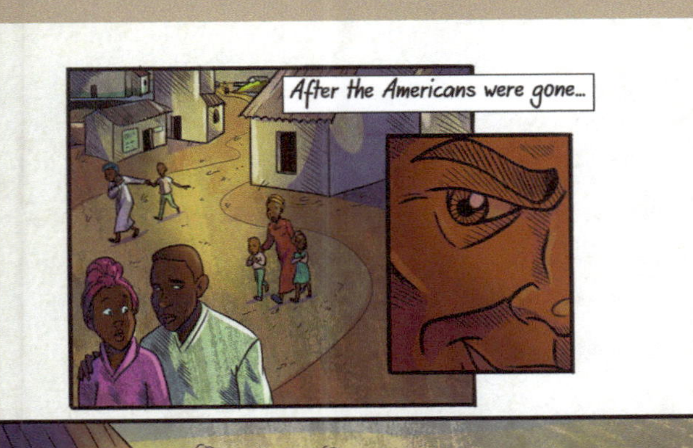

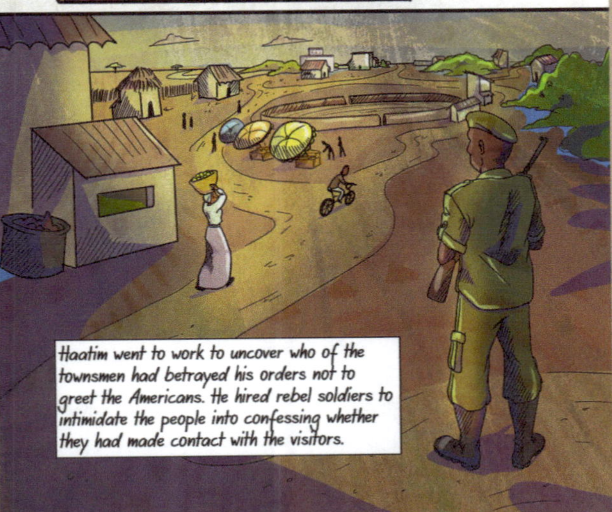

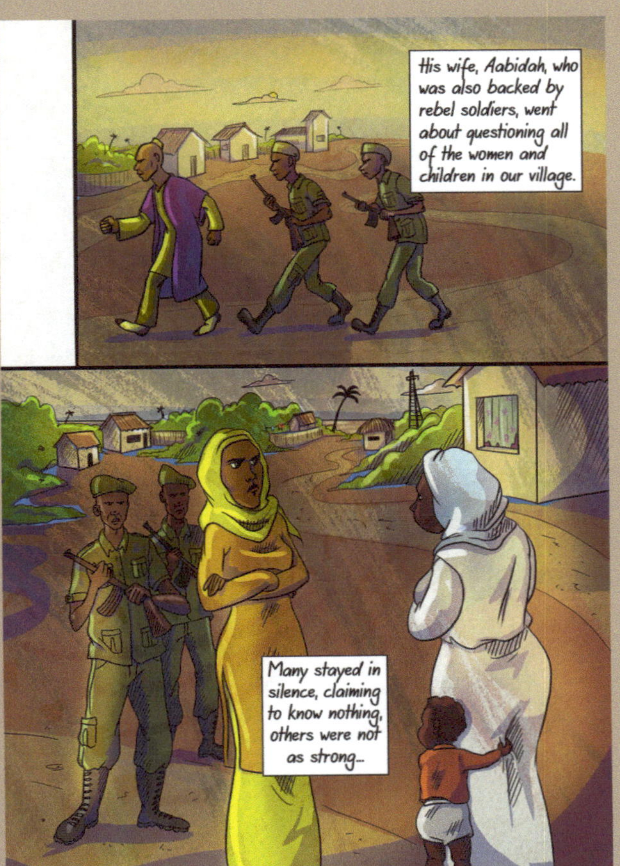

So mama would take my baby sister Hidi and I with her to the place where they sing... a secret location where townspeople who wanted to hear the message of the Wafuasi would go to listen.

Meanwhile Bandele, my little brother, stayed behind to hear Baba's lectures.

Original Spreads

Get Feedback: Reflection Questions

1. Who can you share your work with to get *unfiltered* feedback? Make a list of 3-5 names.
2. It's not all bad! Make a list of 3-5 people in your corner that you can depend on *no matter what!*
3. Are there any artists in your circle with similar goals and aspirations as you? Find a community to build and grow with! BTW, You are **always welcome** at my community **AliciaDianne.com/Community**

It was a cool morning, during the harvest season,

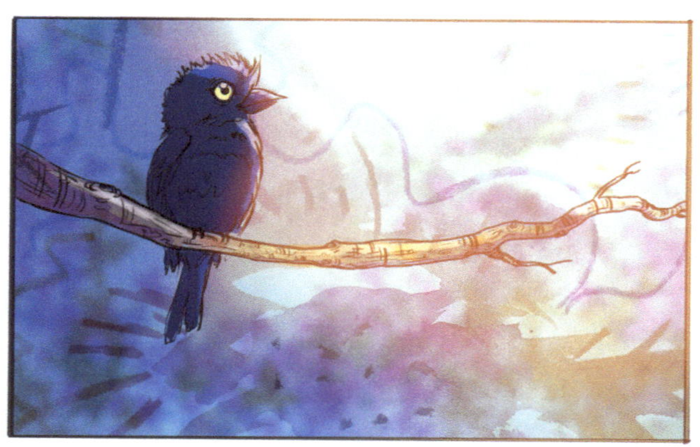

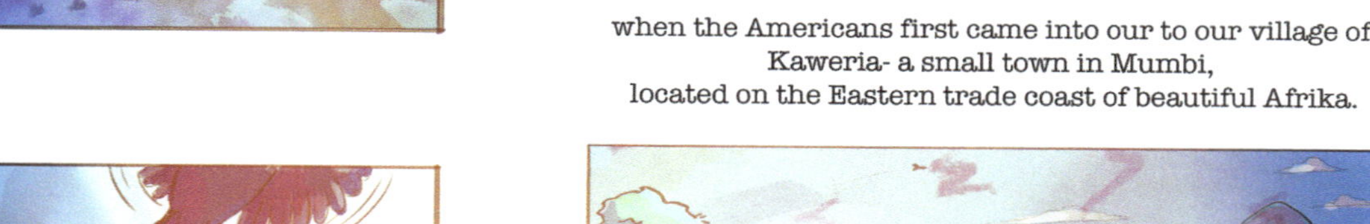

when the Americans first came into our to our village of
Kaweria- a small town in Mumbi,
located on the Eastern trade coast of beautiful Afrika.

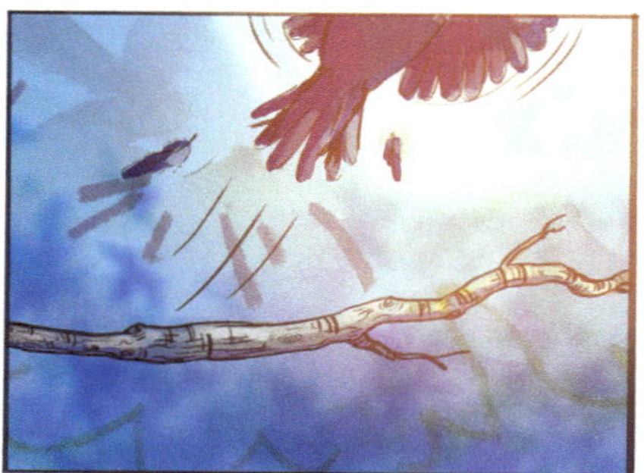

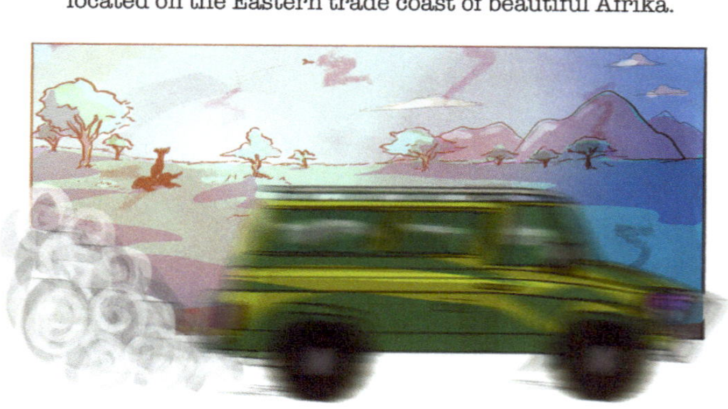

Step 9: Dig Deeper
& Come Back Stronger

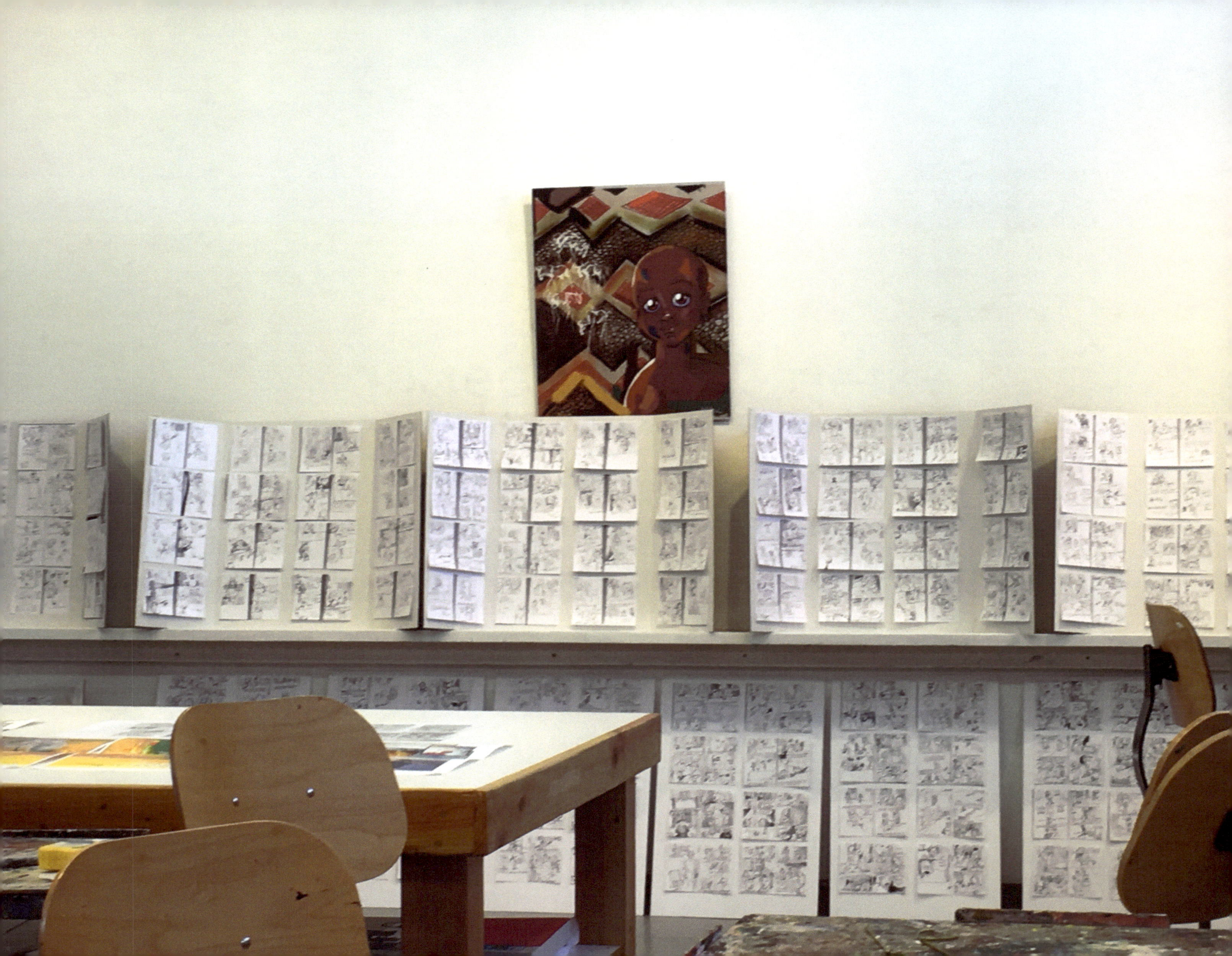

The semester of my first committee critique was a major challenge. Yet sometimes, all it takes is one person to believe in you during the process to make it through. My *Art Critical Studies* professor, Mario Ontiveros, was that one person for me. He gave me the freedom through independent study, to explore deeper into the subject behind my art. He allowed me to pose questions to myself about my art, to ensure that I was saying what I actually felt. It was through his class that I began gaining an even stronger foothold on the information I would need to know to truly tell *Jaydi's Story* in the way it deserved to be told. Likewise, although I didn't want to hear the tough criticism about my writing in critique, I knew that this was still an area l felt insecure in. So even though I believed in my story, I knew it could be better.

Ego is a funny thing. It can puff you up with a false sense of confidence, but once it's bruised, you have to decide between two options. You can either hold onto it and let it weigh you down, stuck on the ground where you currently are. Or, you can choose to *let it go,* and begin to fly! My next step? *Flight.* I sought out CSUN's Head Screenwriting professor. I met with him and stayed in communication with him for months.

You see, there's *always* something you can do. There's always somebody you can reach out to! I didn't know this man, but I looked on the school website, and from there was able to find the screenwriting program, and from there, the head professor.

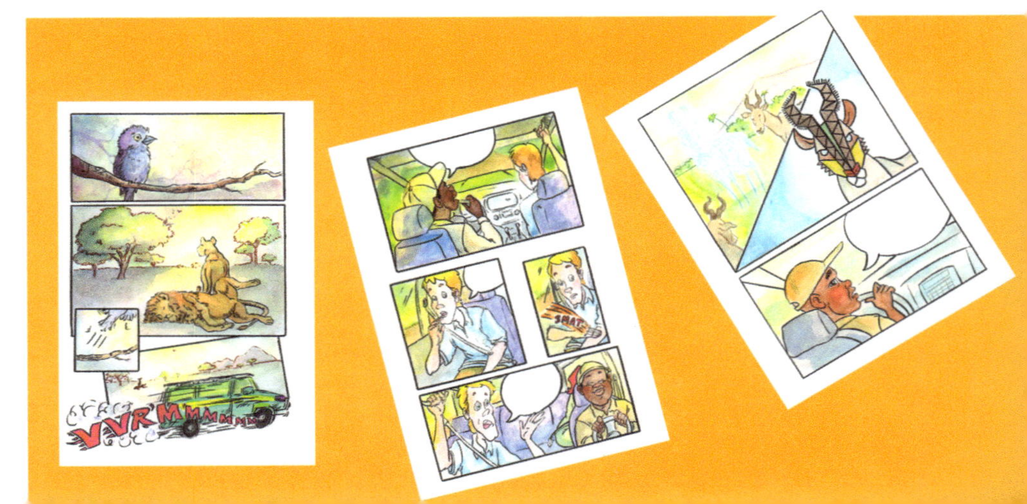

Remember what I said in **Step 1**, *all you have to do is identify one step you can take now, in the present, that will lead you towards your inspiration*. Through meeting with the head screenwriting professor, I was equipped with some great tools that had been missing from my storytelling toolbox. This wasn't about proving anything to my committee, I needed to prove to *myself*, that I knew what I was doing!

```
             Enter… THE SCREENPLAY FORMAT.


FADE IN: INT. AT-HOME STUDIO - DAY


ALICIA enters, she's tall… beautiful and ambitious. She knows what
she wants. She holds in her hands, the scripts from some of her
favorite films, which she's been advised by her new mentor to read,
as well as a copy of "Save the Cat!" A screenwriter's owner's
manual. And… what's that? A subscription to Film Courage - that
cool Screenwriting channel on YouTube…
```

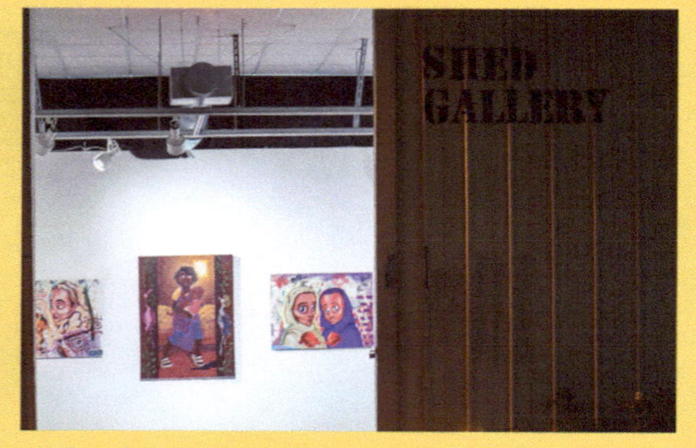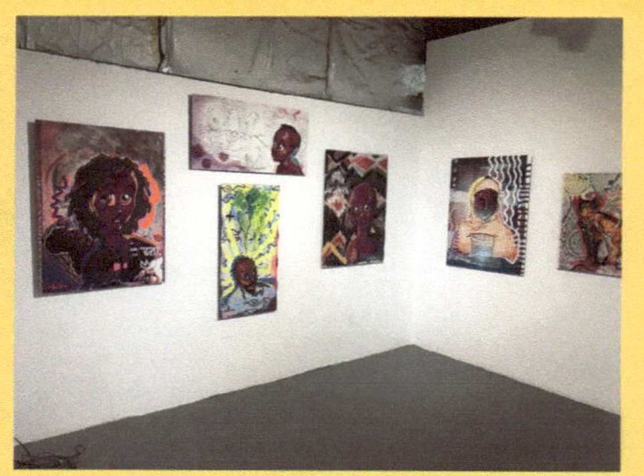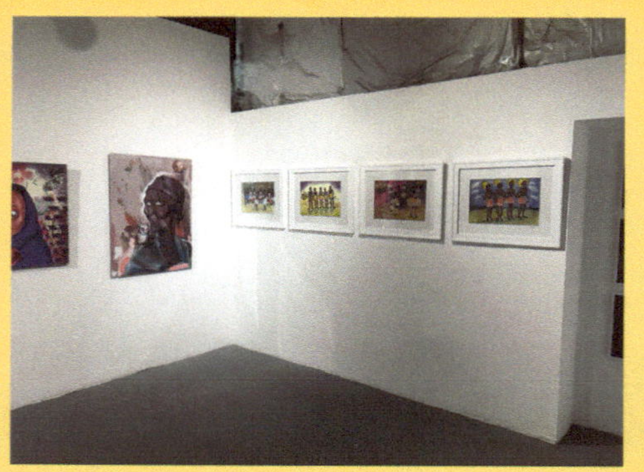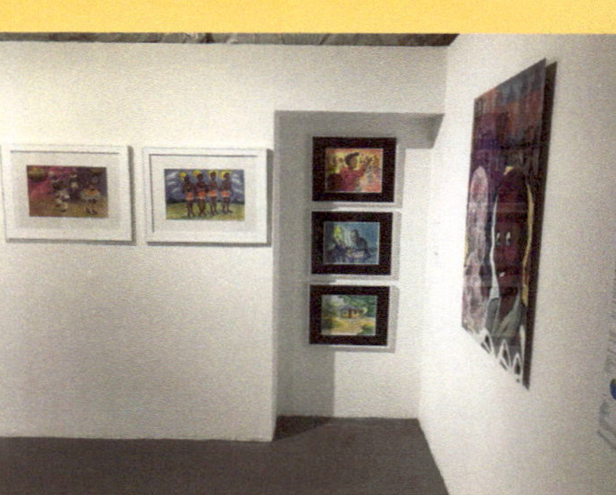

Shed Gallery Show at CSUN, November 2019

The next time I faced the committee, I was prepared. I had completed Draft 2 of *Jaydi's Story*, and later, Draft 3. Only this time, in full screenplay format and with a much greater depth of knowledge for storytelling. As I mentioned before, when I wrote my first draft, my intention was for *Jaydi's Story* to be an illustrated book - and I'd even began the early spreads from that initial version. Now, I had converted the text into a sequential visual narrative. Also, this time in critique, I left out the guess work. Instead of showing just a few spreads, as I had done before, I showed those *Avant-Gardes* my entire *5-chapter collection* of thumbnails! Which I displayed on a number of poster-boards.

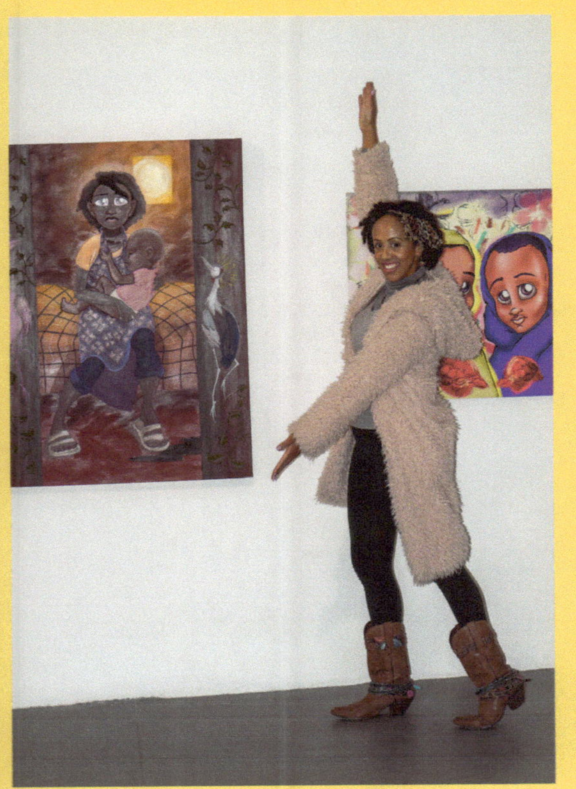
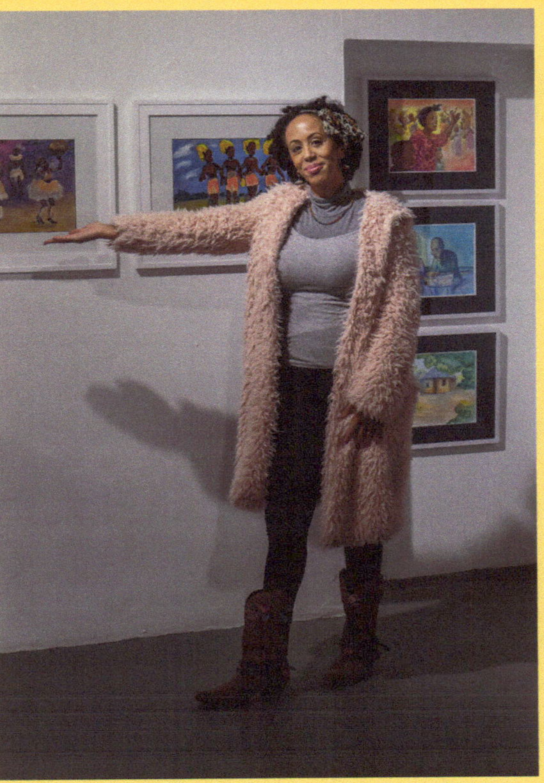
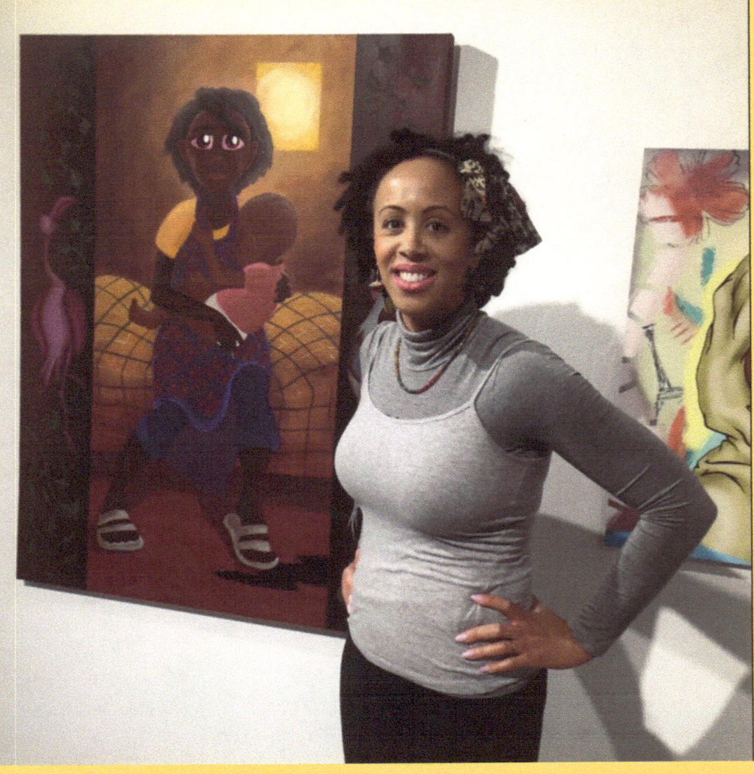

I also hung a large print of my character, *Bandele*, from my *"Inspiration from Kenya"* collection. I had up to this point, decided to illustrate my graphic novel in watercolor and had shown them the latest drafts. I also showed them the visual development art, including environments and Mixed Media paintings. This time, I was also prepared to explain my thought process, and even more importantly, *intellectually defend* myself and my work! Best of all, I had a newly gained, tougher skin! I had found a way to **dig deeper and comeback stronger!** I was ready, if necessary, to handle their harsh criticisms. Which surprisingly, this time, did not come! *Well, well ,well.*

Up until now... I'd studied African History, I'd studied storytelling, screenwriting, and even folktales. But I needed one more key missing piece to afford me the competency I felt I needed to complete my goal! I had to study...

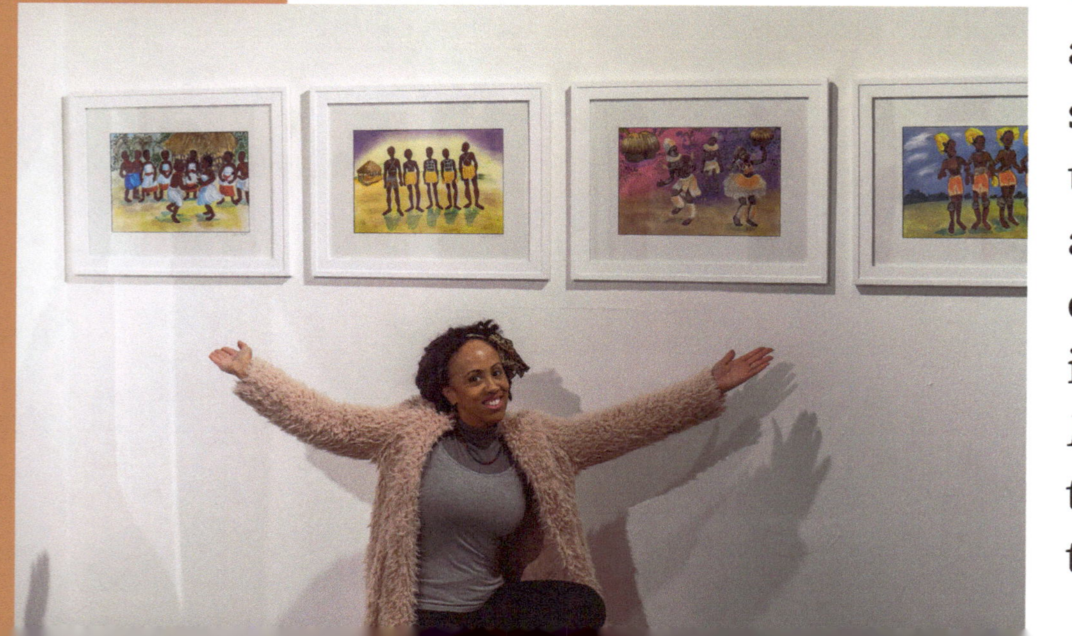

did you guess it? *Comics!* I had learned a ton about animation and it's history during my schooling. Going back to the *zoetrope* and then some! But I was admittedly, ignorant about the history and life of comics. So I decided to do something about it. I enrolled in an introductory class on *Comic Making History*. Through this class, I learned a ton and got to read some fantastic works, too! Like, *The Best We Could Do* by Thi Bui,

Boxers and Saints by Gene Luen Yang, the hilarious *Your Black Friend and Other Strangers* by Ben Passmore, and among my favorite's, the *Akissi* series by Marguerite Abouet. I also learned of some major classics like *The Contract with God* by Will Eisner, *I Saw It: The Atomic Bombing of Hiroshima* by Keiji Nakazawa and the famously banned book in many spaces, *Maus* by Art Speigelman. All of the above of course, are in the *graphic novel* category of comics.

By the way, what's the difference between a comic book and a graphic novel anyway? My favorite answer is this one, "*....About 20 bucks!*" I really wish I knew who said that! Quite frankly, it's true! A *Graphic Novel*, in its essence, is much longer *per issue* than a traditional Comic Book. They're often, but not always, more mature in content.

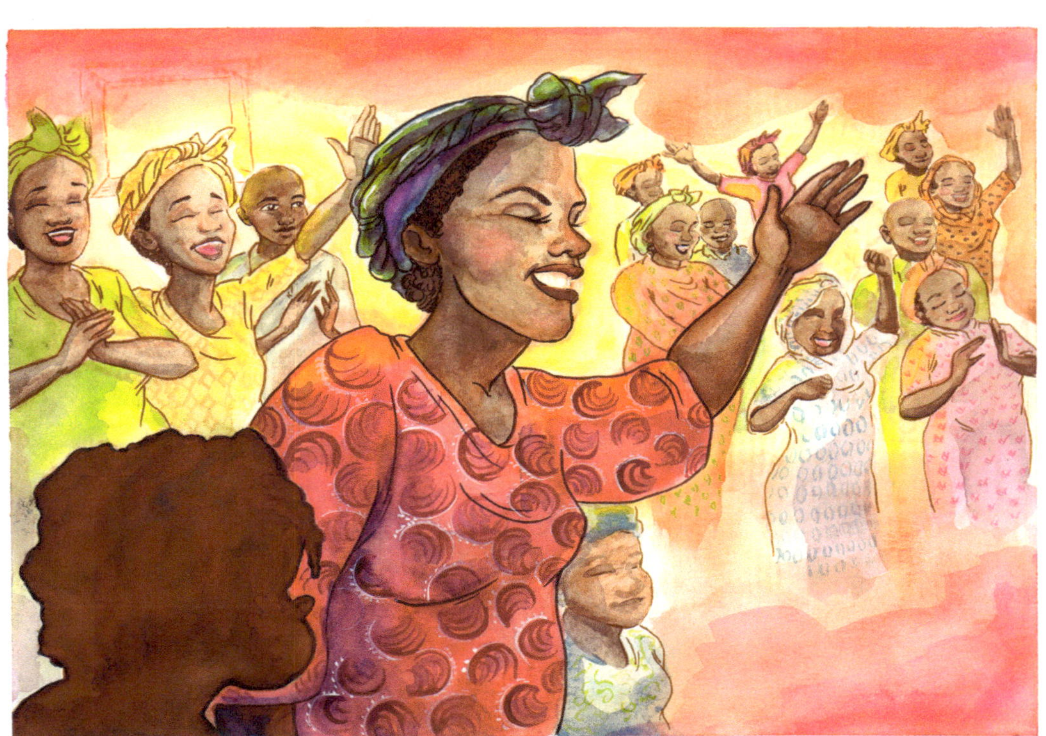

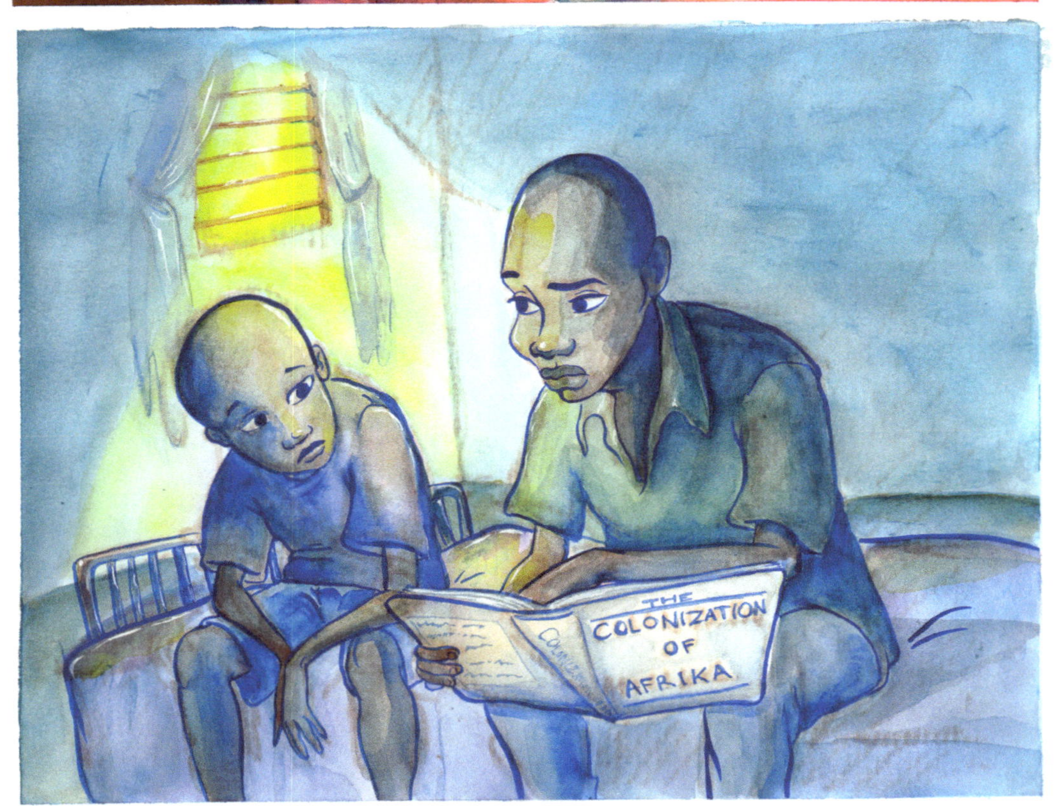

Concept Work shown at Shed Gallery Show

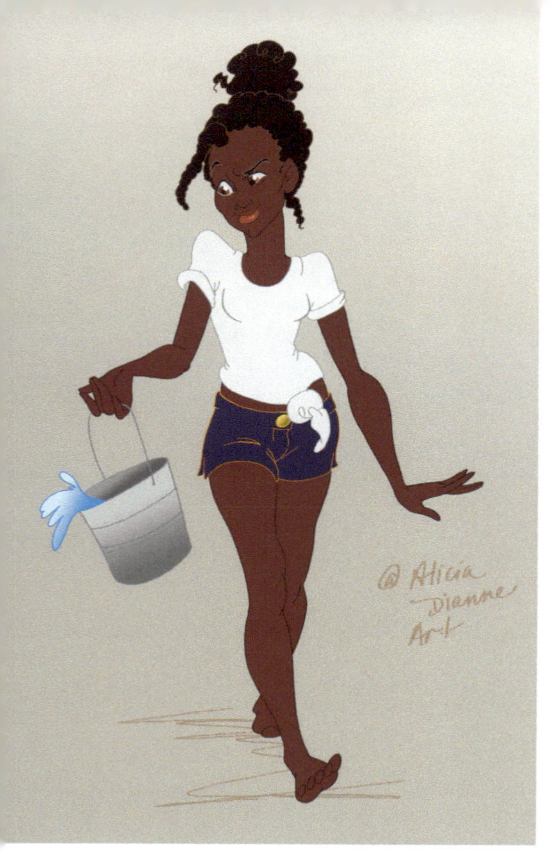

There are comic books, however, in issue count, which far exceed the length of most graphic novel series. Going into the *hundreds* of issues!

A key difference to note, particularly in longer comics series, is that a comic can be carried on by a number of artists as well as writers. Whereas graphic novels are typically the same artist/ writer (individual or pairs) throughout the series. Can a comic series be made by only one artist? Of course! As much is the case for *the funnies* you've come to love in the Sunday Paper. By the way, does *any* of this mean your average comic book a *"lesser art"* than a graphic novel? As my favorite character, Sofia, in *The Color Purple*

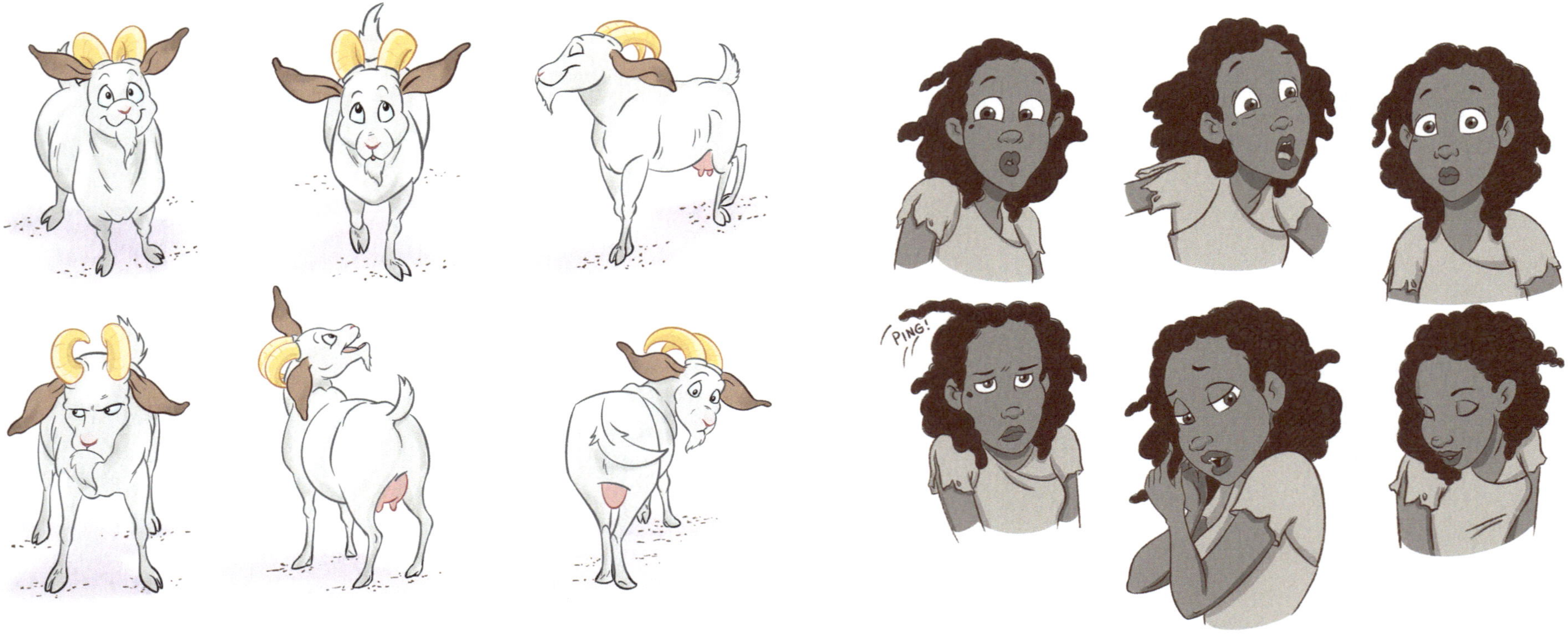

Concepts and final designs of *Jaydi Asha* and her goat, *Atsukpi*

would say, *"Heeeeell no!"* Comic making, as I've learned, is incredibly complex and it takes serious commitment, skill and dedication to make! In *any* form!

Dig Deeper & Come Back Stronger: Reflection Questions

1. Read a book, audiobook, or watch a masterclass on YouTube about writing a screenplay. (I highly recommend *Save the Cat* by Blake Snyder, *Screenwriting for Dummies* by Laura Schellhardt or the channel, *Film Courage*)
2. What movie(s) would you most like your graphic novel to be like? Read the Screenplay! *(Hint: it's more than likely free online!)*
3. Find a graphic novel that relates to the subject matter you are telling (maybe it's one I've mentioned!) Read it and make note of the art style, the lettering, the color palette, the use of dialogue.
4. Write Draft 2 of your graphic novel using screenplay format.
5. Check the **Resource List** for more tools for your journey!

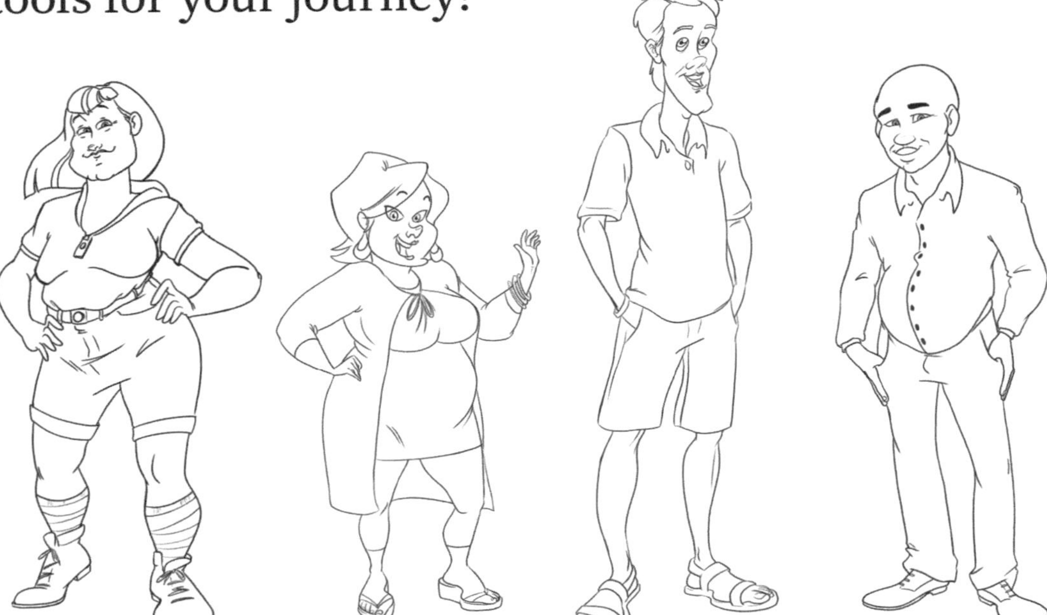

Lineup of *Missionaries* and *Governor Omwancha*

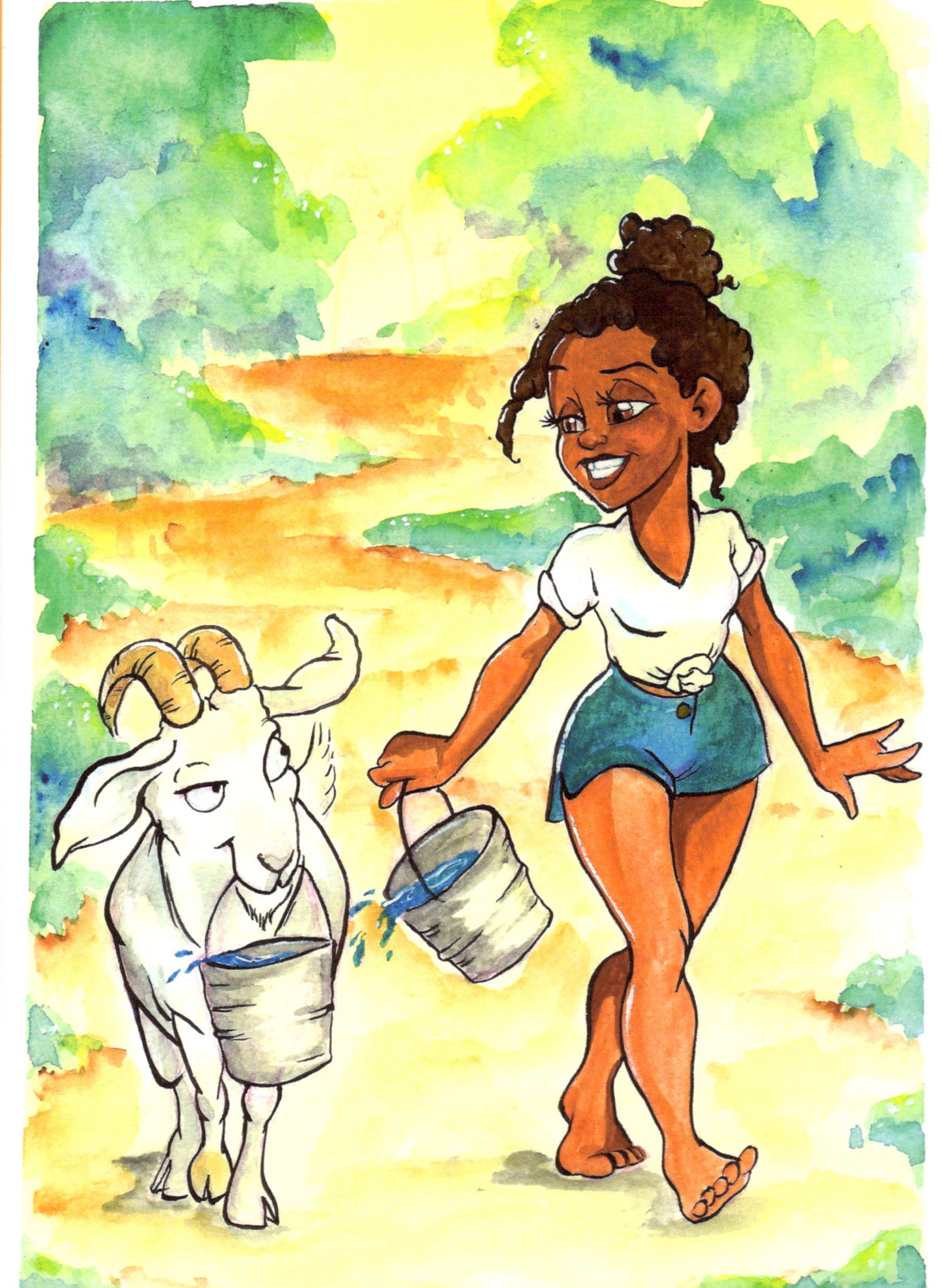

Early concept of
Jaydi and *Atsukpi*

Step 10: Trust Yourself & Push Through to the Finish!

"Making comics is hard!!!" said in the voice of that same lovable *Twenty-Two* from Pixar's *Soul*. (Have you guessed it's one of my *favorite* movies yet?) As I've already explained, watercolor is the world's fussiest medium! So why on earth would I chose to create a comic entirely in watercolor? The short answer, *I don't know!*

The End!

Just kidding… My real answer is, simply because I love watercolor! It is one of my favorite mediums! But in reality, the choice wasn't so easy. I'll be honest, I did initially struggle with wanting to paint *Jaydi's Story* digitally! I wanted my graphic novel to look like a *Brubaker!*

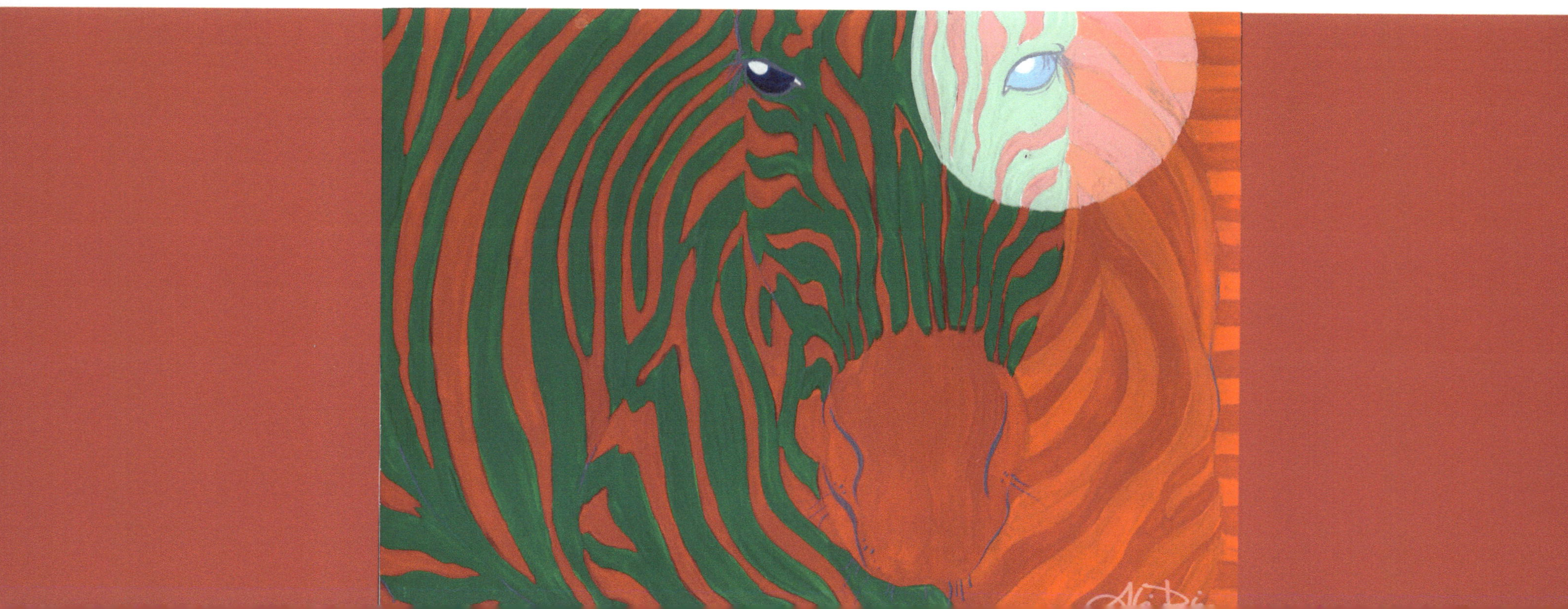

I wanted to *"borrow"* his beautiful way of juxtaposing softness with saturation in all of those delicious digital tones. I've always admired artists who can create beautiful digital paintings. I find it incredible how sometimes you can't even tell whether or not they are digital! They are just gorgeous, seamless artworks that pop out on the screen! At this point in my career, my skill in digital painting was not yet developed. But I wanted *so badly* for that not to be true, that I neglected my own personal strength.

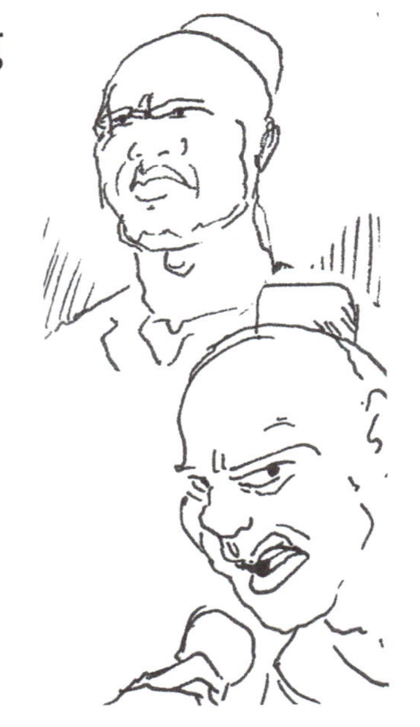

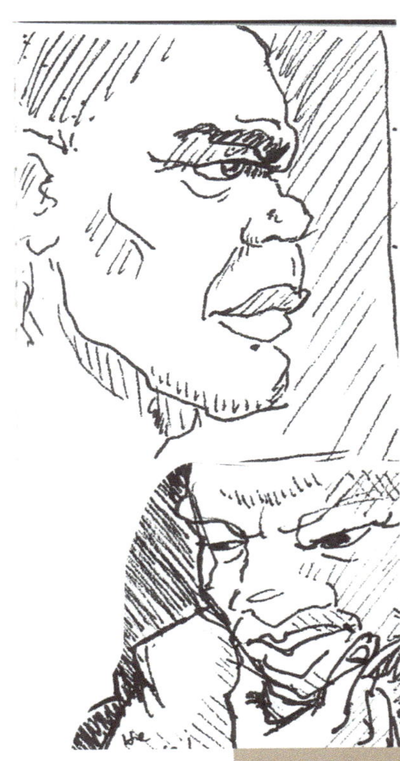

Concepts of wildlife (left) and designs of *Haatim* and *Abida*

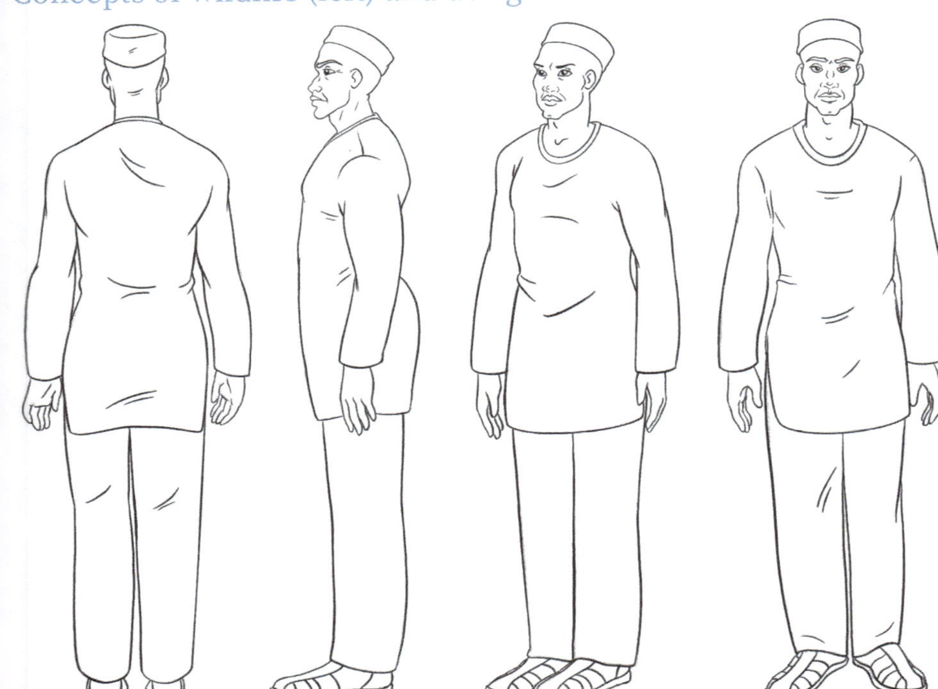

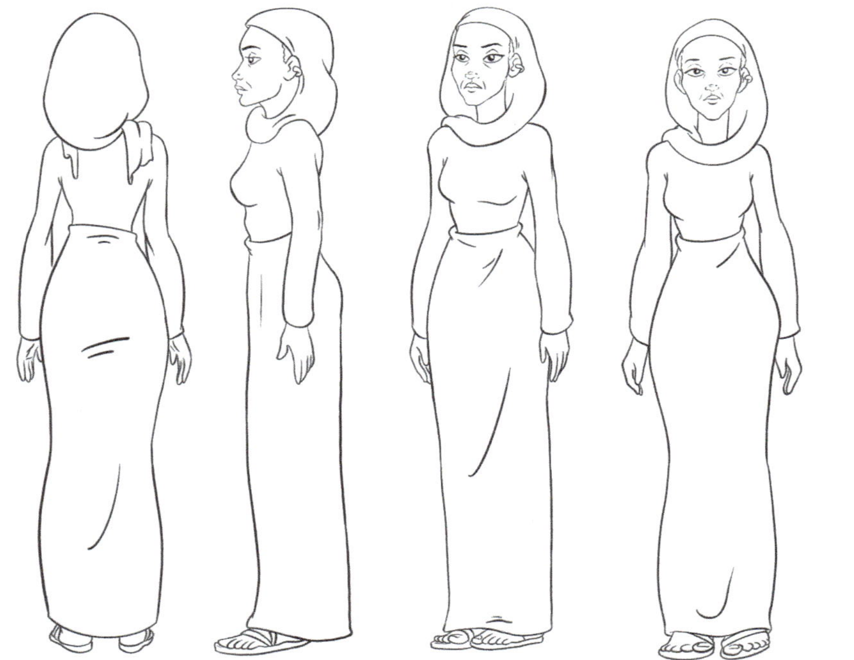

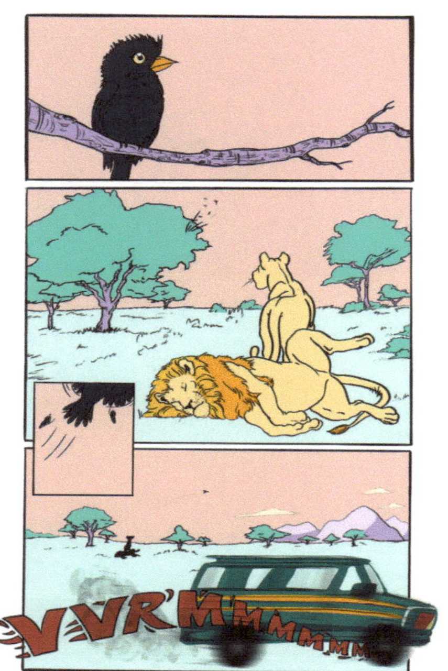

Much like my writing, I was insecure in making permanent decisions for my artwork. I also felt overly influenced by how my illustration professor thought my graphic novel *should* look. So when he suggested that painting my comic digitally would be so much more *"Sleek!… Fast!… Contemporary!…"* than it would be in watercolor, I jumped all over the idea. He fawned, and I said, *"Yes! I wanna be sleek! I wanna go fast! I wanna be contemporary!"* I mindlessly went ahead and completed an entire draft of *In The Beginning* digitally. Want to guess what happened next? I *hated* it! It just didn't have that *"Wow factor"* I was really aiming for. In a word, it *stank!*

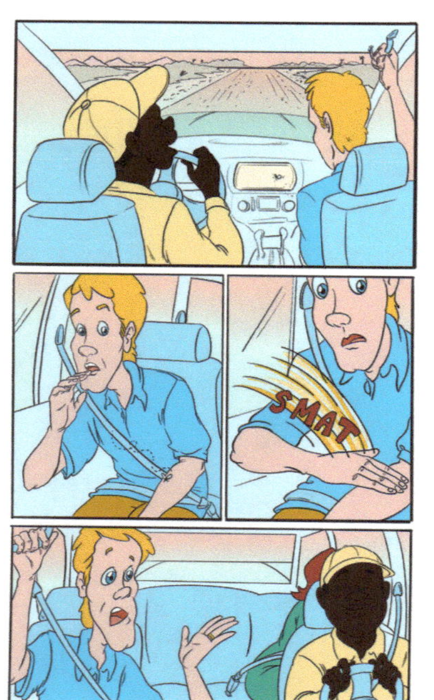

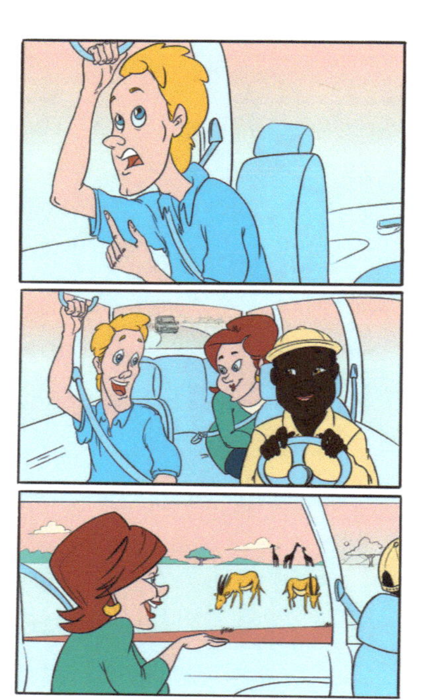

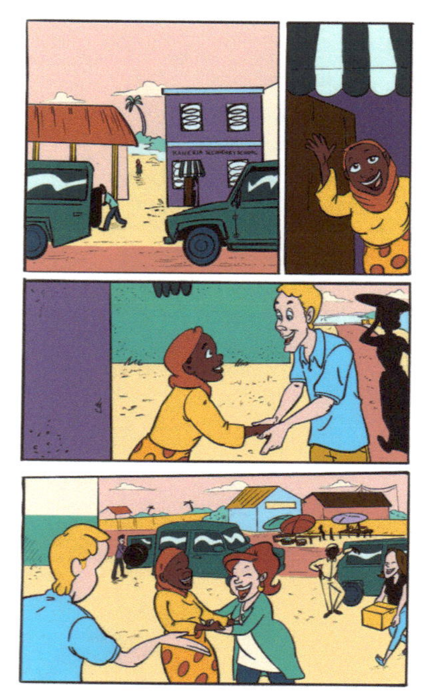

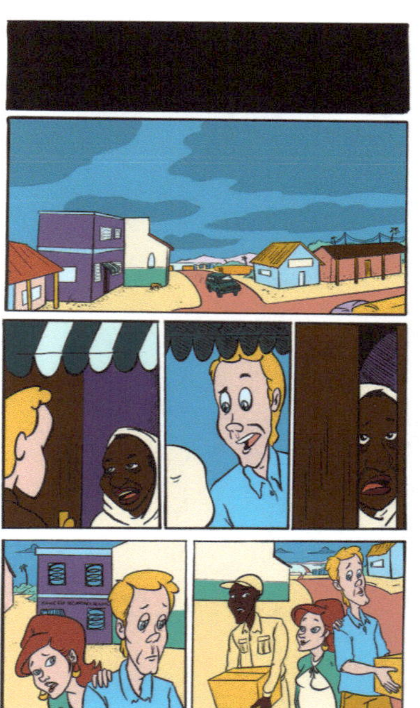

Digital Renderings during final semester at CSUN in 2020

In that moment, I had entirely forgotten the lessons I'd learned previously from Diane, my *Experimental Drawing* teacher. To *work instinctively,* to **trust myself** *and to trust my internal creative voice.* Don't get me wrong, I absolutely love digital painting, and over time, have learned to drastically improve my skill in it. But it just wasn't the right time. I wasn't making *Brubaker* art... I was making a hap-hazard copy. And I *knew* in my heart that it was just simply not the best that I could do.

That Spring semester ended with my professor encouraging the other students to agree that digital was the *way to go!* As for myself, I knew it wasn't quite right. It was 2020, the world was upside down, and my personal life was a nightmare. Facing troubles in my marriage, I opted to stay with my mother temporarily in Smyrna, Georgia, a suburb of Atlanta. By the end of summer, *Jaydi's Story* was officially on the backburner.

Although, there's this funny thing I learned about God. He has a way of speaking to you when you least expect it. A few months down the line, something strange happened as I was writing in my prayer journal. I was still upset because I couldn't release this calling to follow through on the book, I just didn't know how. I couldn't stand the digital paintings I'd made and was so *frustrated* because I just couldn't get them to look how I wanted them to!

That's when God spoke to me, *"I already told you to do them in watercolor!"* He said, totally inaudible, of course, however I felt that impression so quick and strong that I knew it was nothing but God speaking to me in that moment! I shot out of bed. This time, it was more than my *internal creative voice* that I needed to trust! I dug into my box of watercolor paintings, and there they were! The initial watercolor drafts of *Jaydi's Story: In the Beginning* in all their whimsical glory! I knew that was it! No more hesitation! And they definitely had that *"Wow factor"* I was looking for!

Was it going to be easy? *Um... no!* It had been many months since I'd drafted them, and this was before I knew to do the lettering *after* the the illustrations! Most of my drafts were not usable, but I had made a decision! That day, I decided for certain, that I would complete the entire *Jaydi's Story* series in watercolor, and began immediately painting, repainting and inking all of the pages! As the months rolled by I had made steady progress. 2020 had now turned into 2021 and my life had slowly began to take a new turn. My marriage was reconciled and I moved back to California with new found confidence and sense of purpose. I was happy and now, *Jaydi's Story #1* was about 90% complete! What I didn't expect, was the extreme pushback I would feel to complete the remaining 10% of the work.

Most creative people have experienced some form of *procrastination*. It's an ugly word in the Art Community, and one that everybody knows. Have you ever noticed a trend of working steadfast on a project, only to get just about 90% through it, only to start a new project? Sound familiar? What I didn't know, is that this particular procrastinating phenomenon has a name. It's called, *Completion Anxiety*. And *chile*, did I go through it! This is unlike when I was working on my short films or *1,000 Lions*, which actually helped me progress to the first draft of *Jaydi's Story*. This was full-on *Procrastination Overload!* This was the time that my spark had fizzled into a limbo of sorts, where at times I wasn't even making any art at all!

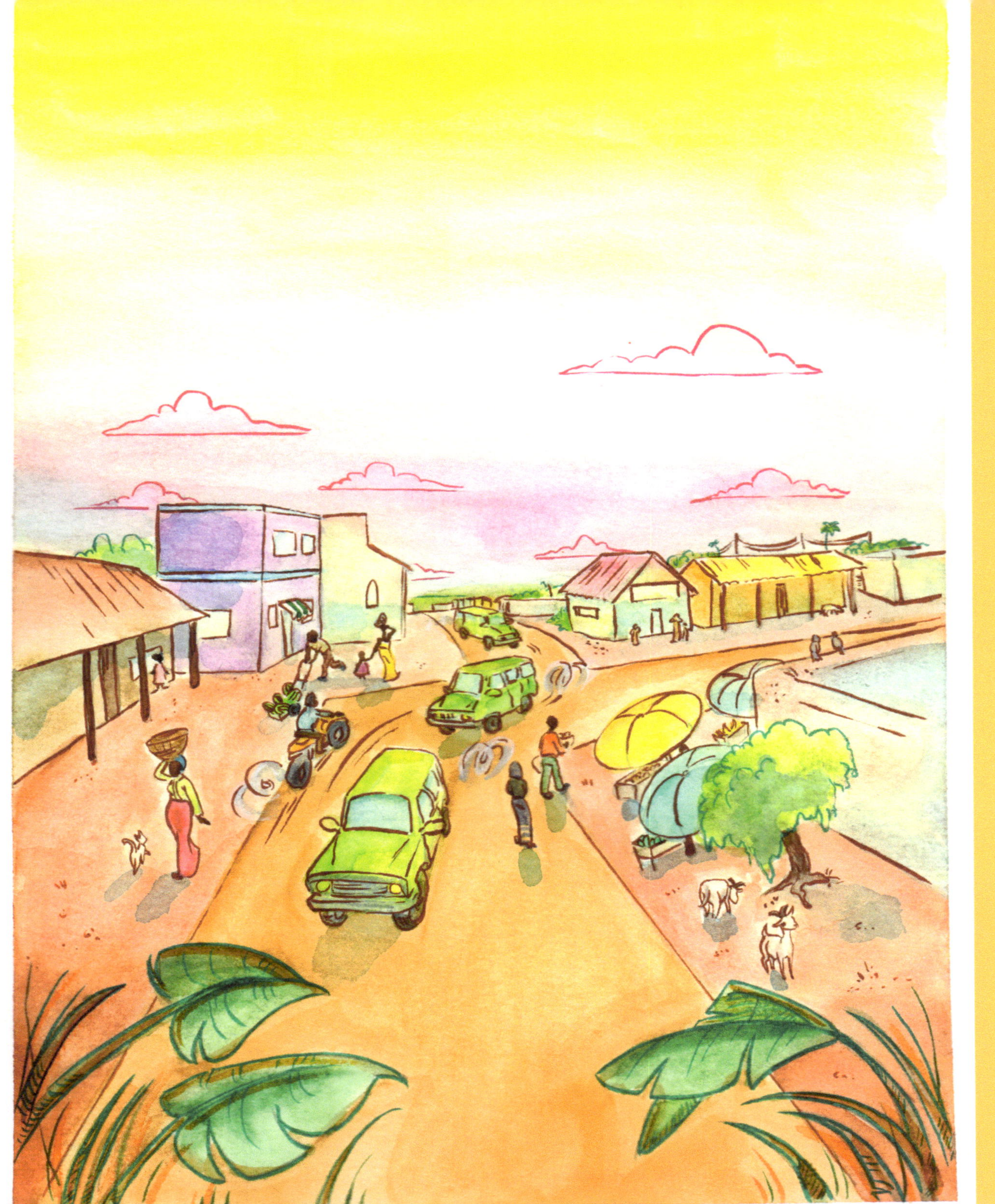

Initial Watercolor

Splash page

For whatever reason, it was really hard for me to cross the finish line and I would realize myself spending days at a time, doings completely unproductive things. Like spending way too many hours on my 8-bit farming game, on a *valley* somewhere. Don't get me wrong, I still love my games. But they have a time and a place. At that time, however, I was completely prioritizing this hobby over my responsibility. Which was to complete the remaining 10% of this book.

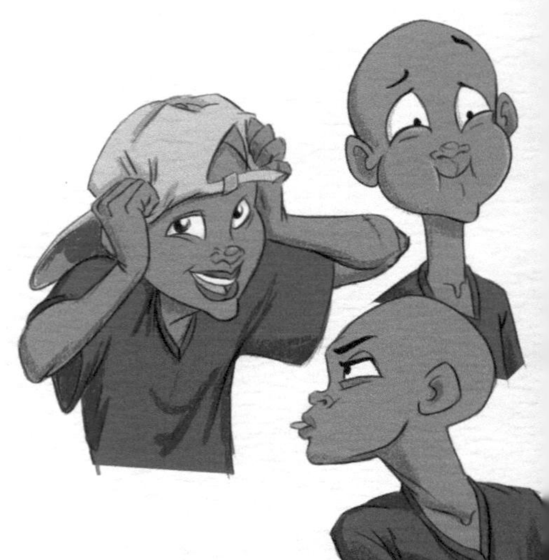

Completing something really important to you can truly be scary. I do think, though, that it's that very first time you do something new, that's out of your current comfort zone (especially something that's particularly *meaningful* to you) that creates the most *internal resistance*. That is when you must **Push through to the finish!** Because you absolutely *can* complete your dream project! Even when you get the urge to *"place it on the backburner,"* (aka quit without the guilt).

Persevere! The internal confidence you will gain in your own competence and ability will be well worth it in the end! Trust and believe! It took me almost the entire year of 2021 to really push myself through the finish line. Looking back, it feels a bit silly, because I know I could have done it in a third of the time.

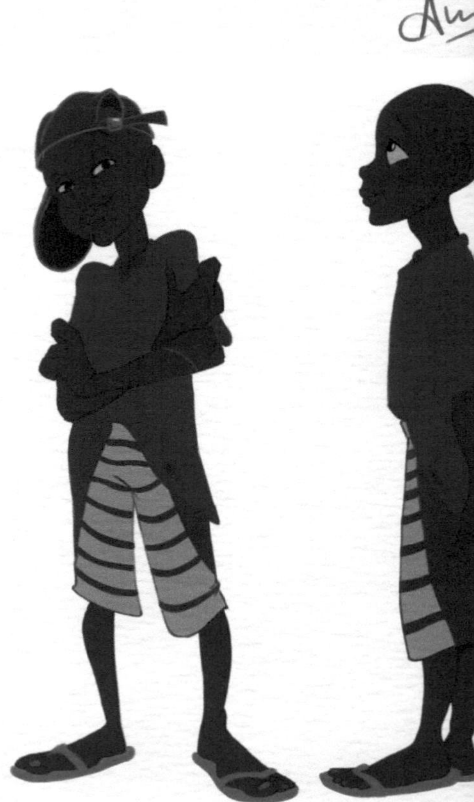

Shoot, looking back since 2015, when I first dreamt of *Jaydi,* if I had known I was making a graphic novel, I could've finished in *at least 2 years,* right? Or could I? My *now*-self could have, but for my *then*-self, it would be impossible! I had to learn all of those lessons along the way to get to where I am now! I had to experience my own *character arc!* I think that's all a part of *respecting the process.* Giving yourself time to grow into something new, while allowing yourself to learn from your *Act 2 obstacles,* of sorts. Remember, I didn't know *anything* about Africa in 2015! I didn't know much of anything about comics or constructing a story, either. I also didn't have the self discipline to write some nearly 200 pages of script, let alone rewrite them 3 and 4 times. I had never been critiqued to tears or experienced the trial and error of the many short stories I'd written. I was *learning* how to be the author I wanted to become, and am still becoming! I had to learn to paint in a way that expresses who I was and am. I was still learning *why* I painted at all! I realize now that when I started, I hadn't yet learned what I *really* wanted to say or what I wanted contribute to the world.

This is the power of faith. For someone like me, who knew nothing, and lacked a clear focus. Someone like me, with no particular ability besides an absolute *love* of drawing and an awe of fairytales. Someone like me, could be heard when I whispered a simple prayer to, *"Use me,"* could be given the strength to dare to challenge myself to make a difference for the sake of what and *Who* I believe in. These are the things that encourage me today. The things that strengthen my faith and make me sit in gratitude. These are the things, that make me sit and think to myself those wonderful words of one of my all-time favorite artists, Elvis Presley, *"My Jesus knows just what I need..."*

Trust Yourself & Push Through to the Finish!: Reflection Questions

1. What medium is your *greatest* strength? Ask 3-4 trusted artist peers (individually) which of your works are their favorite. What mediums were they created in?
2. What art form could you work in for hours at a time and not grow tired of?
3. Create a realistic timeline for you to complete your first graphic novel. Use your previous experience creating pages to estimate how much time you will need. Set a deadline, post it in a conspicuous place, *stick to it* and *re-stick* to it until you're done!
4. Partner with an artist friend you trust. Share your goals with each other and help keep each other accountable!
5. Let me know when you've finished by reaching out to me at **AliciaDianne.com**!

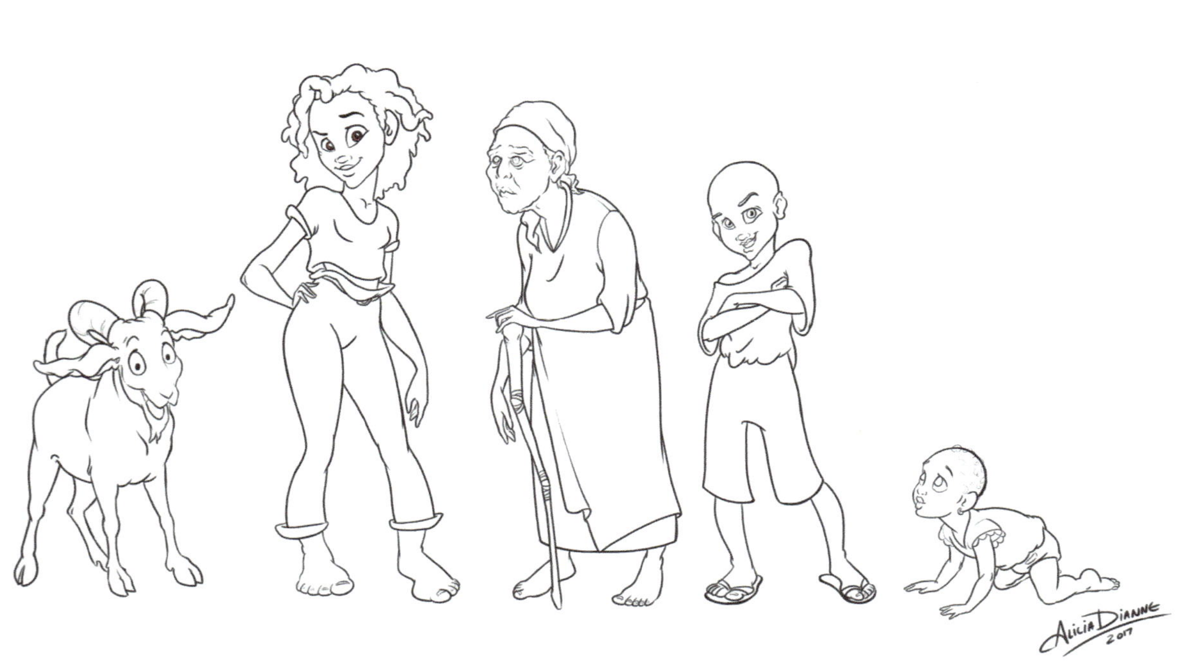

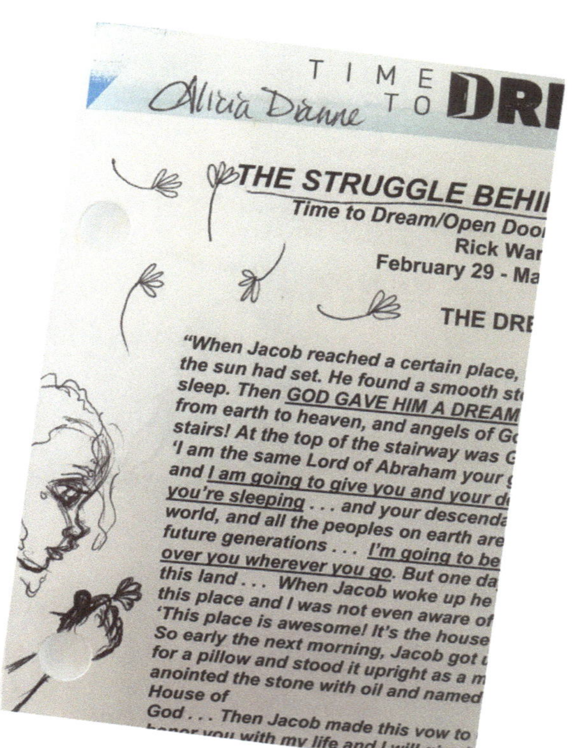

Lineup of *Juma* family (above), discovering final concept for *In the Beginning* cover art on church bulletin and final Cover Art (opposite).

Jaydi's Story
In The Beginning..
Book
1
A GRAPHIC NOVEL BY ALICIA DIANNE

Resource List

aliciadianne.com/resourcelist

About the Author

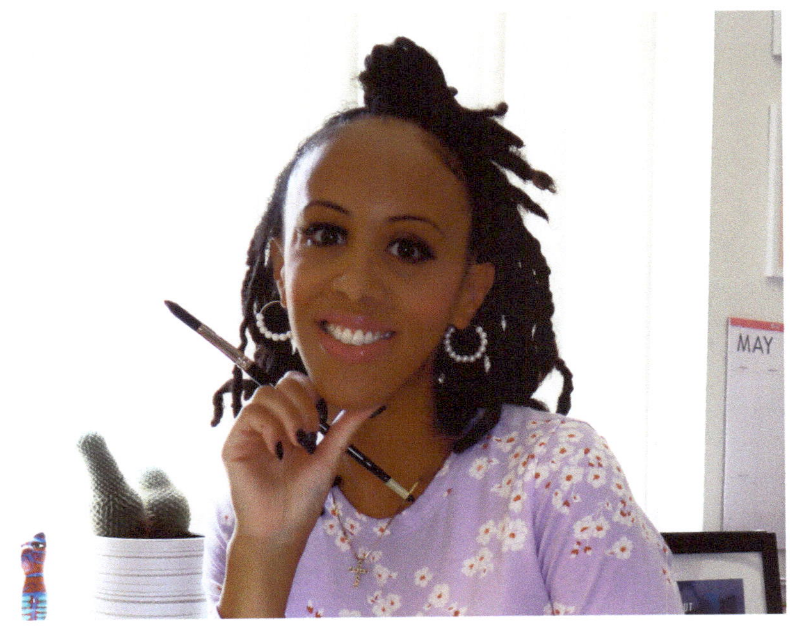

Alicia Dianne is an award-winning animator, illustrator and graphic novelist based in Los Angeles, CA, known for her work in animation, children's books, and storytelling. Graduating with honors, attaining her BFA in Traditional Animation from the School of Visual Arts and holding an MA in Illustration from California State University, Northridge, her art has been featured in exhibitions nationwide. Alicia released *Jaydi's Story: In the Beginning,* her debut graphic novel, in 2021, with the highly anticipated sequel, *Prudence,* arriving in 2026. Beyond her creative projects, she leads artist workshops, teaching art and career skills to enthusiasts of all ages, inspiring and mentoring the next generation of talent.

Learn more about her work and upcoming projects at:

AliciaDianne.com

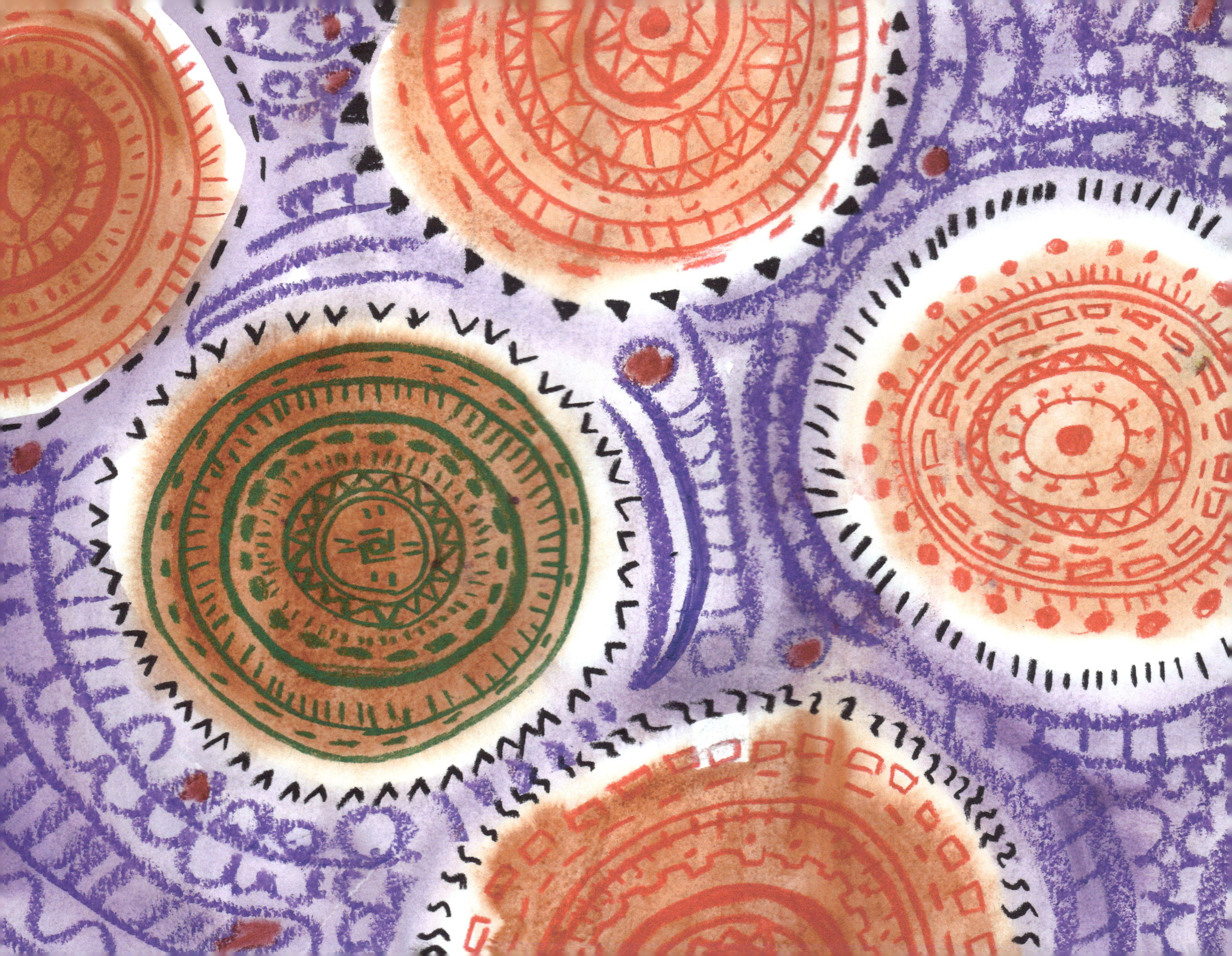